A FARTHING IN HER HAND
Stewardship for Women

EDITED BY HELEN ALDERFER

HERALD PRESS, SCOTTDALE, PA.

CONTENTS

CONTENTS

FOREWORD

ONCE a poor widow dropped two mites, equal to one far-thing, into the treasury. By any standards it was not much, but her offering will never be forgotten; for she put in all that she had.

Every woman must come to a personal definition of stew-ardship for herself. If she sees it only as responsibility, she will be tempted to wrap it in a napkin for safekeeping. But if she sees it also as opportunity, she will open her life to a singleness of purpose that becomes the dedication of a life, a new way of life.

This is the declaration of the Word; that the Gospel is entrusted to persons, to us. Appointed as stewards we become purposefully engaged in mission. Then the goal is not to become simply prudent users of time, wise caretakers of possessions, conservers of energy; nothing we have can be used for selfish purposes but for the Owner. Our response to Him is to use our resources to share the Gospel.

All of the writers of this book are writing from this view-point. They seek to relate the principle of stewardship to life in particular ways, knowing that just at this point of the gulf between belief and practice lies discomfort, but not despair. Aware that it is woman's way to be practical, they go on the rewarding search to close the gulf.

Twelve women have put into words their search in the area of personal resources. In the light of the demands of a secular society, the temptations of self-centeredness, they ask one hard question, "How does God want me to use my resources?"

Helen Alderfer
January, 1964

v

NOT BY MEASURE

Love does not measure gifts to its beloved,
nor count the unrequited gift as lost.
Love suffers all things. Love cannot be moved
from loving by the anguish or the cost.
Love asks not that its loved one's worth be proved,
but gives itself where it is needed most.

So all God is, and has, for thee, to thee was given
when He, for love, bought thee a way to heaven.

Therefore, my heart, reck not the offering up
of thine own self. But freely at His feet
pour thine oblation. Shatter even the cup.
Keep nothing. Make the sacrifice complete.

Only such unreserved devotion is,
in quality, a little like to His.

—Lorie C. Gooding.

1

STEWARDSHIP OF THE GOSPEL

LORIE C. GOODING

THE PRECIOUS OINTMENT OF CHRISTIAN DEVOTION

WHAT great and precious privileges belong to women in the Gospel of Christ! And this is the greatest of them—the pouring out of our very precious ointment which is the love of our very hearts to Him. We are privileged to know Him!

An act of devotion toward Christ precedes every act of love toward one's fellows. This is no minor affection; it is a consecration so embracing as to demand and involve every moment of life, every thought, every act, every known motive and hidden motivation. It is commitment of both the conscious mind and the unconscious to the Lord. If we have voluntarily entered into covenant with God and would attempt to repudiate our vows, He would pursue us as He pursued Jonah, with storms and terrors until we return to Him.

Jesus said, "The first and greatest commandment is: Thou shalt love the Lord thy God with all thy heart and with all thy soul and with all thy strength. The second is this: Thou shalt love thy neighbor as thyself."

Faithfulness in our stewardship requires response to need. The conditions of the world, its crying spiritual needs, its material lacks, its misery and despair, pain, poverty, and hunger all move us to try to alleviate the darkness which surrounds us. Oh, there are times when thoughts of the hopeless, suffering, dying world do burn our hearts with the pity and shame of it all!

1

But this very sympathy sometimes results in an inversion of the first and second commandments. There were some present at the meal where Mary anointed Jesus who found fault with her apparent "waste" of such a preciousness. But she had things in their proper order, and Jesus defended her to them, saying, "Let her alone. . . . She hath done what she could."

There will always be faultfinders. True devotion to Christ will cost you something, and the cost will be great, very precious. Whenever a soul goes deeply into the things of God, when one is taken up and possessed of God, then criticism is inevitable. So many good souls, dear friends, loved ones will fail to understand. Even Christians, with the best of intentions, will deplore the time you spend in reading the Word, in praying, in meditation; "wasted time" that could be used in visiting the sick, helping the poor, or assisting with the mission program.

But all these activities, good in themselves, have no spiritual significance unless they are first bathed in the ointment of worship very precious. Jesus said, "Ye have the poor with you always, and whensoever ye will ye may do them good." But our devotion to Christ is the primary thing.

"And the house was filled with the odour of the ointment." Oh, yes. When the precious ointment of devotion to Christ begins to be poured out, those closest to us will be the first to know. There will be a different attitude, a different atmosphere. Singing will replace sighing; patience will replace quarrelsomeness; grumbling and complaining will be a thing of the past. An emanation of peace and love and gentleness flows out of a transformed personality, and as oil on troubled waters, so it smooths all it touches.

The time of our private devotions is extremely important. This is the "growing edge" of our spiritual life. With the speed and complexity of today's living it becomes increasingly difficult for a woman to claim the necessary time. Always something is pressing to be done. And if we have developed the discipline to postpone the doing, still they run clamoring through our minds as we try to concentrate upon the Lord, and to find His will in His Word. Yesterday's failures, today's

2

duties, tomorrow's portents crowd in upon us and drain off our attention in a hundred little trickles. Until, finally, and without much hope, we send up a spate of words to a God who seems very far off and not very much interested. We feel we are not "making contact" and our prayer is our despair.

There's no strength to be gained that way. If your thoughts are undisciplined, ask Him to discipline them. Don't worry; don't be anxious; don't fret about it. Just wait quietly in His presence. No child of His ever came sincerely before Him in prayer and went away unheard. Remember that He knows your needs and has promised to supply them all. He knows the concern you feel for unsaved friends and neighbors. He knows your heart's desire for a closer communion with Him. He knows, too, your sorrows and griefs, your mourning over your failures and shortcomings. You can't express it all? You don't have to. Be aware of His Spirit within you. Trust Him. "Even the Spirit hastens to help us because of our limitations. For we do not know even what we should pray for, but the Spirit Himself pleads our cause with inexpressible sighing. And God, who searches our inmost hearts, knows what the Spirit means, because He intercedes for God's people in God's own way."[1]

THE PRECIOUS OINTMENT OF "GOOD NEWS"

"Now this is all of God who through Christ has reconciled us unto Himself, and has entrusted us with this ministry of reconciliation, which is this: That in Christ God was reconciling the world unto Himself, not charging their failures against them: and He has entrusted us with the message of reconciliation. Therefore we are representatives of Christ; it is God who speaks to you through us when we implore you, as Christ's spokesmen, 'Be reconciled with God.' "[1]

This is our charge—let us examine it. What is the duty of a spokesman, the function of an ambassador? *He represents another.* When our government sends an ambassador to another country's capital, he represents the United States government. Nothing else. He sets forth the position of the United States government upon issues which mutually affect his country and

3

that to which he is accredited. He does not set forth his private opinion. He does not join in that country's politics, elections, or internal affairs, because he represents an external power. He does not get a job there, or buy a business, or set up in a profession. He does not enlist in the military of that land, nor seek citizenship there. His whole duty is to represent. He takes care that nothing he may say or do, whether in public or in private, can be construed to the detriment of the government he represents.

"Now then we are ambassadors for Christ." We are charged with this representation. Because in Christ we have ourselves been reconciled to God, He has made us His spokesmen. We *must* perform the task. "For preaching the Gospel I can claim no credit. Yes; it is my calamity if I will not preach the Gospel! My willingness to do it is my reward; but if I am unwilling, there is still a trusteeship of the Gospel charged against me."[1] For failure in this, judgment will certainly come. The world needs to know about this reconciliation; that God is reconciled to the world, and all their salvation waits for is their turning to Him who has already turned toward them. But "how shall they hear without a preacher? and how shall they preach, except they be sent" (Romans 10:14c, 15a)?

When God commissioned Ezekiel a watchman in Zion He charged him, "thou shalt hear the word at my mouth, and warn them from me" (Ezekiel 33:7). He further said that the watchman who failed to warn the sinners would be held chargeable for their condemnation. This is a serious matter. Do not think we are excused because we are women. There were women among those who followed Jesus. Not in the inmost circle of the Twelve. It was necessary that these Twelve be all men, as they must constantly live together for the short course of instruction which Jesus had to give them.

But do you remember Martha's complaint in Luke 10:40? Martha was not complaining about that one day's work. Notice verse 39: "Mary, which also sat at Jesus' feet." The word to note here is *also*. In the expression of that day a teacher's pupils *sat at his feet*. Paul later refers to having been "at the feet of Gamaliel." Jesus was recognized as a "Rabbi" or

4

"Teacher." The import of verse 39, then, is that Mary was *also* one of Jesus' pupils. This was a radical departure from the customs of the times. But from what we can know of Jesus' attitudes toward women, it does not seem out of character for Him to accept women as pupils. So Martha was not so much complaining about serving one meal by herself as requesting Jesus to send Mary back to the housework. But Jesus made no difference on the basis of sex in His dealings with persons. Paul recognized this later as he wrote, "So many of you as have been baptized into Christ are clothed with Christ: not Jew or barbarian; not slave or freedman; not male or female; but you are all one person in Christ Jesus."[1] In that "upper room" the women received the baptism of the Spirit equally with the men. We are not told how many women were there, but by the very fact of their presence we know they were disciples of Jesus. Equal empowerment means equal service. The Apostle Paul recognizes this in his famous "veiling" instructions in I Corinthians 11. The right of women to "prophesy" is unquestioned, and "prophesying," understood in the Biblical sense, is not so much "foretelling" future events as "forth-telling" the grace of God.

At any rate, it seems futile to argue over women's "place" in the church. The very first evangelist was a woman! She said, "Come, see a Man who told me all I ever did. Surely this is the Christ!" So persuasive was her "sermon" that people streamed out of the village to "come, see." And it eventuated, as all good preaching should, in their saying, "Now we believe, not because of what you told us, but because we have met Him ourselves!" John 4:7-42. And the Head of the church Himself sent a woman first with the tidings of His resurrection. John 20:17. So we cannot excuse ourselves from this ambassadorship because we are women.

But do not think that even our utmost efforts can save a soul. That is entirely the work of the Spirit. Every one who will be in heaven will be there because of what Jesus has done. The song of the redeemed will be, "Thou art worthy . . . for thou wast slain, and hast redeemed us to God by thy blood. . . . Worthy is the Lamb!" Salvation is of the Lord.

5

But we are responsible that the Gospel of the kingdom shall be preached in all nations for a testimony. Matthew 24:14. So we must make the most of our unique opportunities; *buying up the time because these are evil days.* Homemakers have many opportunities to witness—to neighbors, to delivery and sales people, to visitors in the home.

Professional women meet many situations in which they can witness by word and action. Nurses who care for the ill and dying, and for new mothers, have ready-made chances to present a testimony to their patients and to their patients' relatives. These women often see people during times of grief and real fear, when perhaps the heart is more easily touched than at any other time.

Do not think, 'I am only one. What can I do?" We look out upon the world and see masses of people, lost and dying, rushing to a terrible eternal punishment. And so of course we give of our means. But if money could save a soul, we would stop spending it for *anything else,* and get down to business with our money. The stark fact is: Money just can't do it. Yet money is a part of our total stewardship. But only a part. We have not discharged our trusteeship of the Gospel when we have written a check!

We must stop thinking "people" and begin to think "persons." People are a homogenous mass, like a "herd" or a "pack." Persons are individuals. A mass of starving people in, say, China breaks down to one hundred thousand separate, private hungers. A gang of juvenile delinquents breaks down to 20 to 30 lonely, undirected boys and girls. Statistics concerning alcoholism break down into half a million individual desperations.

Oh, the world is filled with the unloved and the unloving. Prisons are full of them. Streets and slums and country towns are full of them. Hardscrabble farms and great estates and modest little middle-class dwellings have their share. Some of them are extremely defiled, violent, and repulsive. But Jesus said these are the ones He came to call. He understood the principle that the lonelier a person is, the worse he will behave, and the worse he behaves, the more help he needs. O

6

God, comfort the lonely hearts! How much, perhaps, would one friend mean to such persons; one person who would love each of them, one friend in whom he could confide; who would sympathize even when he couldn't understand; who would not turn away from the ugly expression of his loneliness; who would touch him without revulsion.

How hard it is to carry the burden of sin and the train of its consequences which grows greater every day! When Jesus healed the leper, it is recorded that He stretched forth His hand and touched him. Mark 1:41. Think of it! The first touch of a human hand he had felt for years. Kicks and sticks and stones he had known, and harsh words of blame and condemnation. But Jesus dealt with him as with a soul of infinite worth. And in compassion He touched him.

If we are going to be faithful to our stewardship, we are going to have to follow our Lord in meeting people where they are. We cannot hold ourselves aloof from the lepers of our world. We cannot set up churches and expect the world to flock into them. No. We cannot bring the world to Christ. That is too much to ask. The world will not come, and Jesus knew they wouldn't. So our instruction is to take Christ to the world. Jesus said to His disciples, "As ye go, teach all nations." There was no question of *whether* they would go.

And we will have to go, every one of us. We will have to get out of our nice, safe church buildings and go down where the needy ones are. We must not be afraid to go into the ditch and pick up the wounded for fear we will soil our robes. We must not be afraid of befriending the outcast for fear we will be tarred with the same brush. We will be misunderstood, criticized, perhaps even ostracized for our efforts. The very people we are trying to help will often call us "hypocrites," while, for the same action, the mildly religious will say we are "fanatics." We must just learn to "take it."

There are faithful women who have given themselves sacrificially to the service of Christ. They have left home and families, and braved dangers and strangers in their quest for souls to be brought to the Lord.

The American Standard Version gives us this translation of

7

Psalm 68:11: "The Lord giveth the word: the women that publish the tidings are a great host." Dr. Adam Clarke says, "The Lord gave the word: of the female preachers there was a great host." Also in Isaiah 40:9, again we have a woman herald bringing "good tidings," and God gives her the message, "Say unto the cities of Judah, Behold your God!" Dr. Clarke comments, "Such is the literal translation. The reader may make of it what he pleases."

One thing we lack—we have not yet learned how to communicate. We will have to learn to talk with people of different political, cultural, and religious ideas than ours. We must learn that communication is a two-way street. We can't simply present our message; we must learn to *listen*. We are too prone to be transmitters only, having no facilities for receiving. But we must be receptive; we must *listen with the heart*. It is through the hopes and fears, joys and griefs, doubts and convictions of these persons that we will reach them—if we do reach them—for Christ.

We are very highly privileged. God has been so good to us! It is wonderful to be sent to bring the Gospel of Christ to those who need Him as much as we ourselves need Him. It is heart-lifting to hear someone say, "I believe. I will trust Him," and to know that Christ is blessing the work. We must be faithful in our stewardship. And yet, by ourselves, we can do nothing. All of our efforts cannot save one soul.

But Jesus can! He is still in the salvation business! He still saves and heals and empowers! Praise God!

So let us yield ourselves to Him as those that are alive from the dead, pouring out our very precious ointment, breaking even the box, reserving nothing. Love is our stewardship. Love cares. Love serves. Love lifts.

THE PRECIOUS OINTMENT OF FAMILY LOVE AND NURTURE

"The aged women likewise, that they be in behaviour as becometh holiness, not false accusers, not given to much wine, teachers of good things; that they may teach the young women to be sober, to love their husbands, to love their children, to be discreet, chaste, keepers at home, good, obedient to their

8

own husbands, that the word of God be not blasphemed" (Titus 2:3-5).

Here is an area of stewardship tailor-made for women. Older women are not overlooked, as though their usefulness were done, but are enjoined to be teachers and examples to the younger. Grandmothers have a special influence with young children. Older relatives have always served as models for the young. We remember a young girl who, upon being asked by whose preaching she had been converted, replied with the bluntness of childhood, "It was nobody's preachin'. It was Aunt Nellie's practicin' showed me the way." Oh, the fragrance of the precious ointment poured out! A holy life is its own illumination.

Many are the problems and the trials of the young woman through which the elder one has passed. Who can offer help and sympathy better than one who has walked the same road? Sometimes the difference between success and failure is as simple as Grandma Susie's advice to her granddaughter: "You married him for better or for worse, child. You've had the better. Now go back to him, and love him through the worse and the better will come again. And don't forget to pray, child. You'll find it easier to love him better if you pray for him more."

Yes, "to love their husbands." This is a place for the fragrance to fill all the house. Love is a spendthrift. Love is not afraid to give itself away. It gives and demands no return. So women who give themselves for the welfare of others are the world's best lovers. They love their husbands, both the good and the bad. This is no sentimental affection which may easily change with circumstances. This is a deliberate, conscious seeking of the welfare and best interests of the loved one. Many times this love freely given, but at first unappreciated, has at the last proved to be the salvation of the husband. "Likewise, ye wives, be in subjection to your own husbands; that, if any obey not the word, they also may without the word be won by the [chaste] conversation of the wives" (I Peter 3:1). Women are not grudging with their affection. They know how to love!

9

"To love their children." What is more natural? Even an animal loves its young. Our big yellow "Goldie" is instinctively careful with her kittens. But this word speaks of more than a natural love. Pagans love their children; atheists love their children. They bring them up in the best way they know or believe. God has endowed humanity with a great capacity to love. All men love. It is not Christians only who love their parents and their children, their brothers, friends, and neighbors. Then why this command?

Christian mothers are responsible to present their children to God. This is the love which the apostle commands, that they should love their children enough to give them a legacy of living faith which will arm and shield them for time and eternity. In this materialistic age Christian parents have a duty, which is also a privilege, to teach their children that there are values in life which exceed the tangible; that there are precious things which they will never see anyone eating or drinking or wearing or riding or washing dishes in or advertising on television.

We live in an age of rebellion. Children catch the attitudes of their surroundings. So they chafe against restraint and rebel at discipline. They seem to want to be entirely uncontrolled. And it is the tendency of our times to allow them to be so, at least in many areas of their lives. Yet, unconsciously, children need and *want* control. What is juvenile delinquency but the expression by children of their *need* of someone to restrain them, to make the rules and make them keep them? They go to extremes in trying to goad parents or *someone* to *care enough* to lift the heavy burden of too much liberty from their unready shoulders.

Children do not obey unless taught to obey. Christian parents are responsible to teach their own children to obey. Let the child learn early to obey the law of his parents, and the laws of the community will present no difficulty as he grows. Having learned obedience he will not find it hard to yield to the laws of God.

This age has been termed the "age of entertainment." Parents have a duty to God and the child to teach him that enter-

10

tainment and pursuit of pleasures are not the sole end and aim of life.

Parents must work together to accomplish their task. While the children are very small the main burden of it may fall upon the mother, since she is with the children more of the time than is Father. But bringing up a child is a job for *two* parents. It is a full-time job, all day, every day. It can't be achieved by giving it a few hours when we *feel like it*. Careless parents make heedless children.

The home is the place where children should learn to worship. This daily period of worship and fellowship together is one of Mother's greatest allies in bringing up children for God. Children should know the delights of daily worship. They should hear their mother and father pray for them. They should be made aware that God is present at all times and in all places. Children soon learn whether worship and prayer are reserved for Sunday morning church. God will not mean much to them if He is not made relevant to their daily living and their home.

"To be discreet, chaste." This may be rendered, to be wise and pure. This is a facet of our stewardship which attracts but little notice. Yet the odor of precious incense poured out in quiet, well-considered word and love-directed action may penetrate far beyond the walls of the house. Here is where the soft answer may turn away wrath, and the sympathetic tear soften resistance. Here is where the hurtful word may be kept back and a kind word substituted for it. Here friendship and neighborliness may reach out with a pure love and selfless motive, both wise and undefiled, to help.

"Keepers at home." This does not mean "good housekeepers." Neither does it mean "stay-at-homes," as we have been repeatedly assured that it does. Consider the word "to keep" as it is used in its various forms throughout the Bible. "The Lord is thy keeper" (Psalm 121:5). "He that keepeth thee will not slumber" (Psalm 121:3). "That thou shouldest keep them from the evil" (John 17:15). "Who are kept by the power of God through faith unto salvation" (I Peter 1:5).

From only these few examples we can define the verb "to

11

keep." It is a guardianship. So woman is to be "guardian of the home." God has ordained the family, and arranged the positions of its members in such a way that the man usually spends much time away from the home. Being the provider, he must daily labor in the fields of production or do battle in the market places. In the nature of things, mothers spend more time in the home than fathers do. (Working and professional mothers have a special problem in this area, and if they need counsel, they should consult their spiritual advisers.) Mother's influence early directs and motivates. Psychiatry recognizes the formative action of the early years. A certain Catholic priest is reported to have said, "Give me the child for the first seven years, and then I care not what you teach him. He will always be a Catholic." The Bible says the same thing in a different way: "Train up a child in the way he should go: and when he is old, he will not depart from it."

So women are to be "guardians" at home. A mother must maintain the purity of her home. She must be on guard against corruptive influences. She must exercise a censorship over the books, the pictures, the lessons, the records, the radio programs and TV shows, the sports, the places of amusement to which a child is exposed. She should know his friends and his school and his teachers. Sometimes this may be a hard task, and she may not win a popularity contest for it, both among her own children and those of the neighbors. But there will always be faultfinders. A mother has a responsibility before God and she dare not shirk it.

On the positive side of this guardianship we find there must be a definite drive toward God and righteousness. Effort must be made to see that the children have proper instruction, constructive games and toys, educational and devotional reading material that is *readable,* hobbies and activities which will contribute to healthy development of all their abilities. Mother should take part with them in these things. She must be interested to catch and hold their interest. And only interested children will test and exercise their utmost capacities.

Young people need companionship. If there is no organized youth activity in your area or in your church in which young folk can safely participate with profit, here is a ministry which will repay you a hundredfold. Juvenile delinquency would be a smaller problem if parents and churches were *intelligently concerned* for their children. Busy, happy young people seldom get into trouble.

"Obedient to their own husbands." The New Testament has much to say to wives on this controversial subject. But it does say, *Obey*. This does not mean a servile obedience through fear; nor does it give the husband a right to exact a slavish service from his wife in the name of religion. It is, in the main, a legal obedience. At the time of the writing of the New Testament, Roman law was in force throughout the then known world. Part of this law, dealing with women's rights, or the lack of them, was called the *patria potestas*. By this law woman was made a chattel. So long as she remained unmarried she was the property of her father. Should the father die, she became the property of the inheriting male relative. When she was sold into marriage, she became the property of her husband, with the same civil rights as his horse or his dog. He had the power of life and death over her, and, should he be so inclined, could murder her with impunity. On the other hand, the husband was held responsible in law for his wife's deeds and misdeeds. If she were to commit a crime, her husband would be brought to trial, and if the crime were proved, he might well be executed for her guilt. So, in a very real legal sense, the apostle could write, "The head of the wife is her husband" (I Corinthians 11:3b).[1]

Then came Christianity, declaring the equality of man and woman in the Lord. Galatians 3:28. Christ had come and restored (but only in the church; never in civil law) that which Satan had taken away, the partnership of dominion which God gave to Eve equally with Adam. Genesis 1:28; 5:2. There were some women, new believers, who were taking advantage of this "new" status to defy and refuse obedience to their husbands, their legal "heads." This brought the way of Christ into disrepute among unbelievers, who cursed the new belief for a troublemaker. For this reason the New Testament writers plead for obedience and submission on the wife's part

13

("Wives, submit yourselves unto your own husbands, as unto the Lord. For the husband is the head of the wife, even as Christ is the head of the church"—Ephesians 5:22, 23). "That the word of God be not blasphemed."

As good stewards of the Gospel of Christ we should be more concerned about the impression of Christianity we leave with unbelievers than about insisting upon personal rights and privileges. If our consecration means anything, it means that we have given up claim to any personal rights and privileges for the right and the privilege of serving Christ. Thus is the precious ointment poured out.

About the Writer

Lorie C. Gooding (Mrs. Raymond) has several special reasons to be concerned about the stewardship of the Gospel, and particularly by women to women. Converted as an adult, she is fully conscious of the difference the knowledge of salvation through Christ makes in a person's life. Finally, she attributes her conversion to the unassuming ministry of a neighbor lady who showed her the way.

She lives in Killbuck, Ohio, where she faces the problems of homemaking, child rearing, and being a grandmother; her poetry (for which she is best known) therefore grows out of activity, not leisure. Lorie has the happy gift of seeing beyond the usual, the trivial, the temporal to the more abiding values of a thing or an event, but enjoys reasoning through puzzling questions as well. Lorie has one book of devotional poetry published: *Let There Be Music*.

FOOTNOTES

Where (1) appears in this chapter, it indicates either an interpretation or an eclectic translation by the writer, with the purpose of seeking the meaning behind the words of the Scripture. Passages so treated are Rom. 8:26, 27; I Cor. 11:3b; I Cor. 9:16-18; II Cor. 5:18-20; Gal. 3:28.

Much information pertinent to the attitude of Roman civil law toward woman during the first century was gleaned from *The Bible Status of Women*, by Dr. Lee Anna Starr.

14

O LORD beloved, my times are in Thy hand;
My very minutes wait on Thy command.
In this still room, O Blessed Master, walk,
And with my spirit talk.

—Dohnawn Song.

2

STEWARDSHIP OF TIME

ESTHER EBY GLASS

"SO TEACH US TO NUMBER OUR DAYS" (Psalm 90:12a)

THE American housewife is one of the most interesting creatures on earth to contemporary writers. If the articles written about her in any one recent year in magazines and newspapers, to say nothing of books, were clipped, column by column, and the columns pinned together, I do not doubt that they would equal the distance from New York to San Francisco. At least there would be many, many miles of them.

The trouble is, the writers of these many articles don't agree about us. One author will blame all the ills of this generation on the mothers, who, according to his theory, have coddled and spoiled their children, and kept them tied to the maternal apron strings, till they are a race of weaklings.

We open another magazine and discover someone else deploring that mothers spend too much time away from home, neglect their children, and pay no attention at all to them, turning them into a generation of tough delinquents.

Quite often we are labeled lazy button-pushing and gadget-working women, who perform our housework by remote control. In recent issues of nationally circulated magazines writers begin to defend American women as the hardest working women in the world. One man, who has traveled widely, insists that we work harder than our European or Oriental sisters.

To add to the confusion of voices, there are authorities who

17

tell us how to become more efficient by improving each shining moment. We may become liberally educated by keeping a textbook handy, and catching up on our reading if the man of the house is ten minutes late for dinner, or the operator has some difficulty getting the person-to-person call through. We can learn Spanish or knit leper bandages while we wait, or, if we are really efficient, we can do both at once.

This sounds good, until some psychiatrist writes an article warning us that if we don't slow our pace, and spend more time relaxing and just plain doing nothing, we may end up on his couch with the rest of his patients.

This is the babel of voices that surrounds the woman of today as she seriously tries to decide how to be a good steward of the precious gift of time given her by God Himself, in equal portions with every other woman on the wide earth.

"MY TIMES BE IN THY HAND" (Robert Browning)

Before money or possessions there was time, created by God when He divided the darkness from the light. He had the days and nights all ready for Adam and Eve. God has kept right on giving 24 hours daily to every woman from Eve in Eden to Mrs. Present Day in the newest house in Suburbia. She may not have measured her days with hours as we do; she may have used a sun dial or an hourglass instead of a clock if she did measure them.

But penniless or rich, illiterate or a doctor of philosophy, each woman daily sets down the same old problem: a new day to be added to her life, a new day to be divided into fractions. Each evening she arrives at a different answer.

"My times be in Thy hand." So spoke the poet. And so should each Christian woman speak at the beginning of each day.

I like to wake early on a pleasant morning when the birds are twittering and the dew is sparkling and a hush lies over the land. It is easy on such a day to remember that my times are in His hand. It is easy, too, to thank God for another glorious day and to ask His blessing on the hours ahead. Prayer is the natural overflow of a joyful heart.

18

But there are other days when the jangling of the alarm clock jars my already aching head, and before my mind's eye swarm more tasks than any 24-hour period can be stretched to accommodate. Then I find it hard to offer my day whole-heartedly to God, and leave it in His hands. It is as though I am least eager and willing to ask for help when I need it most. Maybe it is because I am not really thankful for the gift of time on the hectic, head-aching days. And this unthankfulness prevents me from putting my times in His hands.

I wouldn't say to the Lord in so many words, "Lord, I have so much to do today that I'm afraid to trust your management. So I'll try to worry it out by myself." But my reluctance to believe He can order my day speaks without formed words.

This is the morning when prayer must be an act of the will. God will honor it no less. He will not turn away when I tell Him that I do not feel the urge to pray, but that I know I will need His presence doubly today.

The first step in the stewardship of time is the simple act of offering each day to God, and thanking Him for the precious hours ahead, regardless of much fine feeling, or no feeling at all! It is the simple setting down of the problem of time which must be worked out during the day.

The weary mother, who has been up and down all night with a crying baby or sick child, may not be able to rise before dawn for a long period of devotion. But a few minutes of quietness before God taken regularly upon rising will be to the day like a few drops of fine perfume dropped on a garment. The fragrance will sweeten the whole day.

Pause briefly to pray a prayer which will include:

Thanks to God for another day.

Thanksgiving for your salvation through Christ, and your past blessings.

Asking His presence through the day.

Committing special tasks to His care. (Mention these.)

Asking wisdom and guidance for decisions which must be made. (Be specific.)

Asking patience for interruptions, and victory over your besetting sins.

(Impatience, nagging, bad temper—each woman knows her weak spots.)

Ask Him to keep you sweet and pleasant all through breakfast and the hurry and bustle of getting your family off to work and school.

This practice of morning commitment takes only a few minutes. God is the originator of all exact scientific laws, but one time He said that a woman who gave two mites gave more than all the rich men who gave great sums of money. Just so with time. A mother, with a large household dependent on her for breakfast and getting off to school, who regularly takes these few precious moments to begin the day with God is giving more of her time than a cloistered scholar who takes an hour for prayer. It cheers us to know that God gets the right answers to our problems of time. With Him one mite plus one mite plus true devotion equals anything.

TWO PLUS TWO EQUALS ANYTHING!

We, the women, are always counting something. We count the silverware as we put it away in the chest or flannel bag after a special dinner. We don't want to lose a single spoon. We count the laundry, making sure every sock has a mate. We count the change in the supermarket to see how much of the grocery money we have saved to stick in the old blue sugar bowl toward buying a new carpet.

We are thrifty housewives who want to take good care of our money and our possessions. Time is one of our most precious possessions.

Although we know that two plus two equals four, yet, with time, as with the widow's mites, two plus two can equal anything when the counting is done with love and devotion to God.

Counting spoons handed down from generation to generation is more than counting spoons. The value of spoons to granddaughter, who remembers when her grandmother used and loved the spoons, is far greater than their actual value on the auction block. The loving concern that each member of the family be clothed in clean garments gives a new dimen-

20

sion to even such an ordinary job as counting laundry. And the hope and love tucked into the old sugar bowl far outweighs the slowly accumulated money for the carpet.

It is even so with numbering our days. At first glance we think this is a problem in flat measurement, but we discover we must use depth measurement, too!

When I was a child I awoke in the mornings with a sense of adventure. Anything could happen! Before the day was done I might find kittens in the haymow, or a hen with a stolen nest of chicks. I might discover the first arbutus of spring, or, while I slept, the frost might have mellowed the persimmons ready for eating. There might be a letter in the mailbox addressed to me, or a new book in the understocked school library. No amount of routine tasks, such as gathering eggs or filling the always-empty wood box, could dim the bright edge of adventure that circled my days.

So many childish traits must be outgrown. But this sense of adventure should be taken out and dusted and put to daily use.

We can wake in the morning to the vision of endless stacks of dirty dishes and unwashed clothes and lunches to be packed and noses to be wiped. Even pulling the covers over our heads will not shut out the picture. Added to a mother's work is the responsibility of the children's tasks. Seeing that Mary gets to her baby-sitting job and Dick to his paper route on time, that Jane practices her piano lesson, and that each child takes her turn at the dishwashing is as time-consuming and energy-depleting as Mother's own work.

"I am both management and labor," one mother quipped. "I manage an establishment, and work harder than anyone else in it."

With a heavy schedule of daily work the housewife, or the career woman, may lose her childhood sense of adventure. But she must not lose the fine glow of wonder. The hours can be added together to equal boredom or fulfillment, depending on individual outlook.

> *Full many a flower is born to blush unseen,*
> *And waste its sweetness on the desert air.*
> —*Thomas Gray.*

21

Full many a bit of glory straight from God's hand is wasted right before our too-busy eyes. Sometimes I have hurried to the mailbox or hung up rows of sheets and shirts without looking about me, scarcely noticing the pear blossoms floating over the grass, or the autumn leaves flaunting their colors in front of my eyes. I was filling my day with work and haste that equaled drudgery. I can do my work just as quickly, and with far more ease, when I take time to absorb the beauty about me while I work. A moment to watch a squirrel or a bird, a rainbow or a sunset, to listen to the baby's cooing or to answer a child's question, can be a moment of wonder.

Right now, outside my window, the meadow is too green to be believable if it was reproduced on canvas. A soft, constant rain has been washing and brightening the grass. God never gives so much beauty to be unnoticed while we slave at our work. He has made our hours so that we can fill them with work, and at the same time fill them with beauty.

We speak of short days and long days as though we did not always count the hours alike. We count them on our tired fingers, or we count them with our thankful hearts. When we add the glow of wonder to our everyday living, we get time and half time out of our days. Two plus two can equal what we will!

$$D = 24h + p + x$$

How many times have you wished for an extra day in the week? Few women voice the lament, "I've got time on my hands," until well past the middle years. Right after the early formula-mixing, diaper-washing years we get into the mud-pie, sandbox, lots-of-laundry years. Then there are the busy school-going, teeth-straightening, piano-practicing years, and the first-date, I-haven't-a-thing-to-wear years. We wouldn't want to miss any of these years, and, most of the time at least, we thank God for them.

The problem of time through all these years remains much the same: how to fit all the work into the allotted number of hours. And it is no secret that there is no simple formula for working out this problem.

A man or woman who has a conviction about the stewardship of money plans carefully in advance how to use his or her income. A certain portion shall be spent for food, for clothing, for recreation, for each need of living. First of all, a stated portion is reserved for the Lord. Without a plan there is likely to be nothing left for the cleaning bill, or only a nickel for the collection plate.

A plan is just as necessary for the best use of time as for the best use of money. $D = 24h + p + x$ is simply saying that Day equals 24 hours plus plan plus all the unknown and unexpected interruptions which you know will come your way.

Sometimes we cast nostalgic glances back to Grandma's day. Grandma's work wasn't easier, but her obligations were more clearly outlined for her. She was expected to keep a clean, tidy house, cook and wash and iron, pamper Grandpa, bear and bring up his children, spank them when they were naughty and praise them when they were good. She raised chickens and vegetables and flowers, baked and butchered and canned and preserved, dried corn and apple snitz, made soap, went to church on Sunday, and to an occasional quilting party or wedding or infare.

Our grandmothers usually planned their time something like this: wash on Monday, iron on Tuesday, mend on Wednesday, weed garden on Thursday, clean on Friday, bake on Saturday, go to church on Sunday. Sometimes the mending day was also a day to go visiting. Grandma frequently took her sewing or knitting or other handwork along with her, and needles flew in time with the tongues, and the afternoon was pleasantly filled with double measure.

Grandma may have taught a Sunday-school class, or baked a cake for a church social once in a while. But no one asked her to assist in a cancer drive, or collect for the welfare fund or Red Cross, or serve on the program committee for the PTA, or run for president of the Missionary Society, or be a youth leader, or plan a rummage sale and collect and sort rummage for the Fire Company Auxiliary, or help with a chicken barbecue for the benefit of the local hospital, or donate cakes and fancywork for relief sales, or chauffeur children to swimming classes, or prepare a paper for the book club, or sing in

23

the community or church chorus, or. . . . I could go on and on, and as you read, you are probably amplifying or revising this list.

It is in the face of this multitude of extra demands on a mother's time, all worthy enough, added to her already over-flowing schedule of regular home duties, that a woman must come to some decision about what her first and most important obligations are, and try to find a reasonable, workable plan.

No one woman can devise a plan for another with much success. But it should be a weekly plan covering the same main household chores that Grandma listed, although we may not use the same days she used for the tasks. The plan should be simple and flexible, and will need to be changed from year to year to fit the family's needs.

Added to the master plan there are several simple helps which lessen confusion and wasted time, especially as the children grow older. One is a weekly list posted in some conspicuous place, on your bulletin board, or on the wall near the telephone. On this list appear, in order, each day's extra jobs and engagements, complete with times and places. A glance in the morning reminds Mother that Johnny has a four o'clock dentist date, Dad a trustees' meeting in the evening at the pastor's home, and the clothes for relief are to be collected at the door in the afternoon.

Another confusion- and time-saver is a calendar, with large spaces, hung on the wall beside the telephone. An engagement book is not quite as satisfactory, unless it is firmly fastened so that it cannot be carried upstairs or stuck under a pile of papers. As invitations are accepted, or appointments are made, they can be marked at once on the calendar. And a glance at the filled space keeps one from promising to chauffeur children to the spring musical program at school and help serve supper for the Golden Year's Club on the same evening.

In our family, Mother's lists are a standing family joke. But they are a standing source of satisfaction, too, when any member forgets which day he was to pick up the picture proofs at the studio, or where the Youth Fellowship is having the next meeting.

24

A good plan contributes to good stewardship of time, but it is a means to an end, not an end in itself. It is altogether possible for a woman to become a slave to her routine.

"I can't possibly go along to help clean that house for the refugee family if you go on Monday," Martha will say. "I always wash on Monday." Another woman could never help with any church or community project on the day of a weekly neighborhood sale which she attended regularly.

A plan is intended to be a good servant that helps to save time and keep the household running smoothly. It can become an exacting master that robs the housewife of freedom to serve anyone but her own family.

To be an efficient housewife does not mean to always wash on Monday, or even to get every corner cleaned and every window washed each week, although this is a fine ideal to keep on the master plan. The Christian housewife must learn to rearrange her planned work many times to include entertaining unexpected guests or canning perishable fruit or caring for a sick child. Each woman has 24 hours a day, but that is all she does have. The best of management can stretch time to include only so much work, and sometimes regularly scheduled jobs must be done in short order, or even be let slip by undone for a week.

Conscientious young housewives, in their anxiety to be perfect housekeepers, wives, and mothers, are likely to set goals of perfection so impossible to reach that they carry a needless burden of frustration. Good stewardship of time does demand good planning and diligent work. Just as indispensable is the ability to accept a degree of inefficiency with good humor, when visitors, broken equipment, or other interruptions cause performance to fall short of the perfect plan on paper.

Many high-sounding words can be written about stewardship, but the subject is really tied to the most commonplace concerns of everyday living. Our time is divided between living with our families, working for our families, and reaching out to others about us.

We would probably all agree that living with the family comes first on a mother's list. But it's so easy to push just living into a corner for tomorrow, or later on, or when the work is all done. Tomorrow is too late to cuddle the baby, tell stories to the toddler, help the first-grader with his lessons, listen attentively while Junior describes—with gestures—the no-hit, no-run game he pitched, lend a shoulder for 15-year-old daughter to sob on: "Mother, I could have died! Not one boy even spoke to me at that drippy old party."

It isn't just a matter of spanking the naughty and praising the good. We have to do that sometimes, too, but we need also to try to understand and meet the needs of our children at each level of life. It takes time, but it is time well spent, to read a good book telling the development of the child, what to expect of a two-year-old, a four-year-old, and on up the line.

Preoccupation with the children sometimes causes us, as women, to forget that our first obligation and joy is to live in harmony with our husbands, and take time to keep alive the love on which our homes are founded. This provides the atmosphere for the home, and has a profound effect on the children's welfare. If our houses are in a sort of muddle when the children are small, we can correct that as they grow older. If we can't keep the weeds out of the garden in late summer because we are too busy canning and freezing vegetables, we can plow the weeds under in the late fall.

The children won't really care too much about a bit of disorder or a few weeds; they may not even remember these later on. But the memory of an atmosphere of warm love and happy voices, of laughter and gentleness and tenderness, will remain with them and make them strong, happy people later in life. Love between husband and wife needs daily attention; upon the pillar of this love the home is built.

Harmony is never, or seldom, achieved without thought, and the expenditure of time. The easy harmony of colors in a beautifully decorated room is not the product of using only one color, but colors that complement each other. Harmony in music isn't playing just one note, but notes that blend. And

26

in each case, a master hand has worked. So harmony between husband and wife doesn't mean that these two will echo each other's ideas or ditto each other's words. It is a skillful blending of two lives to make an interesting pattern of family living. And this is worth all the time it will take. Especially, it needs the constant direction of the master hand of God, the author of love.

We should sometimes ask ourselves whether we are doing our share in adding beauty to the family pattern. Have I taken time, for instance,

To listen, really give my attention, when my husband tells me about his work, or his hobby, or some meeting he has attended?

To thank him when he has gone out of his way to fix or build or buy or paint something for my use, or my pleasure?

To praise his thoughtfulness to the children?

To compliment his appearance when he is carefully dressed to go away?

To go somewhere, and enjoy something, with him alone, without the children once in a while?

To apologize, and ask forgiveness, when I have spoken hastily and unkindly to him?

To tell him how much I love him?

One day the children will be gone. We must take time to build companionship that grows stronger and more congenial through the years.

Along with living with our families, we must, of course, be working for them. There is no way to keep a house orderly and clean except to keep cleaning, room by room, day after day, week after week. We have better equipment for cleaning than Grandma had, but we still sweep and dust, polish and wax, till the finished job leaves us aching in muscles and inwardly glowing with satisfaction.

Many household decisions involve both the stewardship of money and the stewardship of time. For instance, in buying clothing for our family we must consider dollars and cents, but we must also keep an eye open to the time that will be spent in laundering these garments. Washing is at best a

27

weekly job; for some women it is almost a daily one. And nothing accumulates more easily than the pile of ironing. One should decide whether to buy drip-dry garments that may require more care in laundering, but little ironing, or more sturdy fabrics that can be thrown in any type of washer but must be carefully ironed. The answer will depend on your family's need and preference, but it is only right to remember the time involved.

I have always been a little perturbed by speakers who lay down ironclad rules for ironing sheets, or not ironing sheets, for starching pillow slips, or not starching pillow slips. Many factors, such as the age and size of families, decide such matters. When my mother was an elderly shut-in who spent many hours in bed, I ironed her sheets and pillow slips as beautifully as I could. But I simply folded and smoothed with my hand the sheets that went into the beds for the rest of the family, every one well and strong and usually asleep as soon as his head hit the pillow.

Stewardship involves saving time; it also includes using time kindly and well.

The virtuous woman of Proverbs arose early and gave meat to her household. Christian women are usually known to be good cooks, and rightly so. Good stewardship would certainly include using our talents to cook food that is well seasoned and nutritious and attractively served. A question might be raised about the too-frequent serving of rich desserts that take much time to prepare. Sometimes cooks, poring over cookbooks or magazines, need to pray: "Lead us not into temptation."

Somewhere between the perfectionist and the slattern stands the housewife with an understanding of the stewardship of time, who runs her house as a trust from God, and does not allow it to run her.

The Christian woman gladly gives time to her church. And she will want to co-operate in some of the activities of the school and the neighborhood. But it is entirely possible to become so involved in committees and drives that one has a meeting scheduled nearly every night of the week, spends hours baking cakes or collecting money for charities, sits up far into the night preparing papers or balancing accounts for organizations. Here indeed is a problem in the right division of time.

The church holds first place. We must never neglect it for other areas of service. We want to attend the regular services, and take our children with us. We want to serve wherever we can, but when the children are small, a woman should not feel guilty if she cannot teach a Sunday-school class, sing in the choir or chorus, accept an office in the Women's Service organization, and be a sponsor of the youth group. No one person should serve in so many capacities at one time anyhow, but in small groups a capable woman is often asked to carry an intolerable load of responsibility.

Good stewardship would indicate that a woman serve where her gifts and training will count most for the good of the church and the work of the Lord. A trained or talented singer should choose the choir. The Sunday school will probably be the avenue of service where the kindergarten or elementary teacher can contribute most. A woman with experience in working with young people is needed to work in the church's youth program. And almost every woman has a gift that can be used and should be used in the program of the church. To fill one place well is good stewardship. A single woman, or a woman whose children are grown, can easily take more responsibilities outside her home. But it is good for a younger woman to keep some activity also, where she can exercise her talents in the Lord's work through the church.

A mother needs to take an interest in the school. She should take time to learn to know her children's teachers. Whether our children attend public or church-sponsored schools, we can go to PTA meetings, and discover some of the strong and weak points of the school. No woman wants to be a self-appointed critic, but we can work through existing groups such as the PTA to correct bad situations, and to build better libraries, and facilities for special education for handicapped children. We need to take an interest, keep informed, and help when we can.

Our communities need hospitals, heart clinics, facilities for treating crippled children, fire companies, organized charities. Our church sponsors campgrounds, children's homes, old people's homes. Almost all of these worth-while services have women's auxiliaries; they could hardly operate without them.

Here is the place for the woman to exercise stewardship by learning when to say "Yes" graciously, and when to say "No" firmly. We do have an obligation to these worthy institutions; we would not want to live where they were absent. If each woman would try to serve in one community auxiliary, this might provide relief for the overworked women who belong to too many. It is as hard for some of us to accept as it is for others to refuse requests. One woman said she felt like a pie cut in six pieces that had to serve ten people. When we have taken on too many outside activities, then, by the process of elimination, we should narrow our field to include only so many as we conscientiously feel need our participation. No one woman can fill all the needs for help.

The modern world does offer one choice to homemakers that Grandma seldom had offered to her, the choice of a job outside her home. This is particularly attractive to women trained in the professions, teaching, nursing, secretarial positions. During the years that her children are small, a mother will want to be with them. She might do some substitute teaching by the day, or some small jobs of typing at home, if she wants to keep her fingers in her profession. My neighbor, a registered nurse with three children, gladly gave my mother injections when she was suffering from shingles. She said she liked to keep in practice, and her competence was a comfort to me.

A mother must ask, "What would God consider the most important use of my time just now, when my children are small?" Would I be dividing this time aright if I divided it between my home and my job? And there may be different answers, but a woman would want to consider the question seriously before she decided.

A QUESTION OF TIME

There are other questions that women raise about the use of

30

time. I offer these for our thinking, not because I can furnish answers.

One of my friends asks why we are always busier on Wednesday evenings than any other evening of the week. She has decided Satan fears the prayer meeting, poorly attended though it may be, or he would not put forth so much effort to get people to think they are too busy, or too tired, to take time for the midweek meeting. Is it good stewardship of time to plan ahead for prayer meeting, even though husband and wife may sometimes take turns attending, if there is nothing planned for the children? she asks.

Another problem in stewardship of time is the innocent-looking phone hanging on the wall. It is at once woman's best time-saver, and her worst time-waster. A good study can be made by keeping account for one week of the actual length of every phone call, and then striking a grand total. The answer can be a revelation.

There is a feeling about that women enjoy raising money the hard way. We will bake cakes, make aprons, or gather rummage for sales, our critics say. But we hate to dig down and donate actual dollars and cents. In the days when a woman's nest egg came from a nest of eggs, she often had little to offer but her eggs. These same eggs, worth only a few cents a dozen, were worth considerably more baked into a cake or custard pie. The baking was a labor of love; the whole transaction involved sacrifice and giving of self. In the present day of cake mixes and commercial bakeries and joint checking accounts, some people feel the situation has changed. How do we decide whether it is a better use of time to donate a cake, or give a donation of cash?

If we live in a neighborhood where everybody spends much time keeping their lawns immaculate, shall we be careful to do the same? If the neighborhood women or the women of our church always serve elaborate company dinners that take days of previous preparation, shall we do the same? How much shall our stewardship of time be influenced by local custom, or the opinion of other people?

Some women are concerned about our pattern of entertain-

31

ing. We need time for friendship, time to keep old friendships warm and to cultivate new ones. How much time should we spend entertaining our relatives and close friends? how much becoming acquainted with our neighbors and casually inviting them into our homes that we may know them well enough to speak with them about spiritual matters?

And isn't it odd that when Cousin Sophie, who always rubs us the wrong way, and speaks condescendingly of our furniture and children, is coming to visit, we spend much time getting ready? For her, our most disagreeable relative, we will spend hours polishing the silver, waxing the floor, ironing the curtains. We plan mouth-watering menus, formal table settings.

But for dear Cousin Grace, beloved by all, we simply put clean sheets in the bed, dust hastily, and add another can of mushroom soup to the casserole! We don't spend much time for her; it's the time with her that gives us so much pleasure. What motivates this difference in our use of time? Good stewardship?

When I was a girl, a favorite rhyme in the songs we sang was shining and repining. Christian women are tempted to waste much time repining that might be better spent shining. God must feel sad when we throw away precious hours in inordinate grief for dead friends who are happy in His presence, in remorse for sins of the past that He has freely forgiven, in excessive worry for the future as though He could not take care of us.

The temptation to worry about the past and the future is intensified as the passing years empty our days of much of the routine work that has occupied us. We can accept these as burdens or blessings.

I learned wisdom in this area from my mother and my mother-in-law. My mother-in-law saw, within a 14-month period, three of her seven children marry, another son leave for college, and her youngest start to school. Her household shrank at an abnormal rate. My mother lived 27 years after the marriage of her youngest child, who was born to her when she was 45 years old.

I think of them often now, as I prepare to move from our

32

ten-room farmhouse into a five-room house. Within this year my mother, who lived with me as a shut-in for seven years, and my mother-in-law, who lived nearby, have both passed on to be with the Lord. Our daughter was married this year also, and our son contemplates alternate peace service next year.

"You'll be lonely and wonder what to do with your time," people warn me. And I remember my two mothers, who were diligent in working for their families, who gardened and butchered and raised chickens and churned butter. But, when they laid these tasks aside, they accepted the extra hours with gladness.

They now had time to read, to write letters to old friends and distant cousins, to take a nap in the afternoons without apology. Mother Glass had more time now to play the piano, and Mother Eby got out her paint brushes, so long idle, and took up her painting again. If friends dropped in to chat, there was no longer necessity to keep an anxious eye on the clock. They could even take trips to visit their children, or to see historical landmarks, or attend church meetings, with only one suitcase.

My fondest memory of each is much the same, Grandma Eby in her armchair by the window, Grandma Glass on her porch rocker, each with her open Bible.

When one has done her work well, she can let go of the busyness of the middle years without regret, and with a certain relief. A life lived for God pays compound interest in old age—serenity and confidence and joy.

We all know happy old couples who enjoy their later years together. But statistics point to the fact that women, in large numbers, outlive men. Unmarried women and widows dominate the feminine portion of our older generation.

Not all of these women are able to live in their own homes or the homes of relatives. To be good stewards of our older years, we need to think clearly and plan as concretely as possible for these years before they come. Especially important is developing attitudes and habits that will make us not only adaptable to other people, but able to draw on our own resources for long hours we may have to spend alone.

Women hesitate to take time for themselves. But if we are to help others, and be ready for the older years, we must take some time to fulfill our obligation to ourselves as persons, and our personal obligation to God.

We live in a world of hurry, bustle, confusion. Our radios, record players, television, stereo and hi-fi sets bring us much diversion, entertainment, news, beautiful music. Even farm wives sometimes forget to listen to the birds, the crickets, the water running over the stones, the voices of silence. We forget how to be quiet, how to be still.

Lately I attended a women's retreat. The director of the retreat, a missionary who never raises her lovely voice, said to us: "This is a retreat, a place where we do not say, 'Listen, Lord, for Thy servant is speaking,' but, 'Speak, Lord, for Thy servant is listening.'"

I want to tell a little instance from this retreat. One hundred women sat together one morning, sang together, prayed by turns, shared their burdens. Then our leader told us: "At home you often have no time for a really quiet time; so often the telephone, or the doorbell, or the baby interrupts. Today we will have a 30-minute quiet time. No one will speak to another, but we will each find a quiet place to read and pray alone."

I sat on a stump in the woods. It was quiet. Occasionally a bird called, a twig snapped. I opened my Bible. It is my practice to read my Bible through, one time after another, not hurriedly, but regularly. I was reading in Ezekiel on this day, and this verse stood out:

"Yet will I be to them as a little sanctuary in the countries where they shall come."

I thought on that. I thought of the world today, torn by strife. I thought of the rising tide of communism, of the plight of Christians in Red China and all iron curtain countries, of the surge of nationalism in African countries with its problems beyond human solution. In our own country, race violence, juvenile delinquency, fear of war.

Then I read again: "Yet will I be to them as a little sanctuary." This was promised to the Jewish captives, who had been torn from their homes, who had seen things too terrible to remember, and who were still in exile, lonely and afraid.

The words spoke to me of my personal obligation to commit myself and my family to God, who will be to us a little sanctuary. This obligation means I must take time each day to hear God speak. I can't wait for a retreat once a year, although a retreat fills a special need. We do not regret the time we spent each day, when our children were small, reading a short portion of the Bible and praying with them. It was not always easy to take the time; they were not always enthusiastic about it, although often they were. Now they are grown, and we are glad for each link we forged in the chain of family devotions.

But how much we have to contribute to our homes, our communities, and our nation will depend almost entirely on the quality of our inner lives. We need to bring to all our work a calmness, a lack of fear, a humility, that comes only from personally knowing and listening to God.

This means we must take some time to grow as women. I offer these suggestions for growth, as a necessary facet of stewardship of time.

Set aside a short time—you may not find a long period—to switch off the music, and read quietly your Bible, or a devotional book with printed Bible portions. Pray. If you aren't good at praying aloud, lift up your heart to God. He reads hearts as well as words. Just ten minutes, or 15, or 30, while the children take their naps, or right after they have all gone to school. Set a regular time, and keep it conscientiously. This can be your little sanctuary.

I know there are women who read many books, no matter how many children they have or how much canning they do. Others just don't take time. Now, magazines and digests fill a good place, but to grow as a person, read a book sometimes. If you are a nonreader, try reading three or four books a year to begin. Pick a good religious book for women; you will be surprised how much you will enjoy Eugenia Price or Isobel Kuhn or Amy Carmichael. Then to stretch your mind, read

35

a good missionary book, and one of the interesting new biographies or travel books.

Listen to good music. Then, sometimes, turn it all off, and listen to God's flutes outside your window—the birds singing with ecstasy in the spring mating season, the drowsy hum of bees on a warm summer day, the frogs and crickets in the summer twilight, the swish of the wind through the dry autumn leaves, the fury of the storm in winter.

Listen, though your hands are busy washing dishes or pulling weeds. And as you work, open your heart to God—God who so loved that He gave His Son, and who still so loves that He gives peace and calmness in the face of all the anxiety that surrounds us today. He will be a little sanctuary for us in the place where we are.

In the final analysis it is the quality of our living that determines our attitude toward stewardship of time. It determines whether we look about and see obligations to others, or opportunities to serve others; whether we think of time as a cup to empty, or as a measure to be filled; whether we meet the tensions of everyday living with fear and bitterness, or with courage and faith and that calmness that comes alone from a heart at peace with God.

"Live life, then, with a due sense of responsibility, not as men who do not know the meaning and purpose of life but as those who do. Make the best use of your time, despite all the difficulties of these days" (Ephesians 5:15, 16, J. B. Phillips).

About the Writer

Esther Eby Glass (Mrs. Forrest) was born in Denbigh, Virginia, the sixth of seven children. She lived on a farm, near the Warwick River, near the woods, and is still nostalgic at times for Tidewater and pine woods. Before she married Forrest J. Glass and became a farmer's wife, she lived eight years in cities. They have two children, Virginia and Richard. Since her first story was printed 15 years ago she has written more than one hundred stories and articles, a booklet, *When*

You Date, a chapter for the devotional book, *Breaking Bread Together,* and three books in the *Miller Five* series for juveniles. Since the death of her parents and the marriage of their daughter they have exchanged their ten-room farmhouse for a five-room ranch-style house.

RELEASE *your child that he may go forth and live.*

—Phyllis Martens.

ON THE BIRTH OF A CHILD

Lo—to the battleground of Life,
  Child, you have come, like a conquering shout,
Out of a struggle—into strife;
  Out of a darkness—into doubt.

About you the world's despair will surge;
  Into defeat you must plunge and grope—
Be to the faltering, an urge;
  Be to the hopeless years, a hope!

Be to the darkened world, a flame;
  Be to its unconcern, a blow!

—Louis Untermeyer.[1]

3

STEWARDSHIP OF CHILDREN

PHYLLIS MARTENS

EVERY time a baby is born, the intense drama of an immortal being begins.

Our little ones: the crown of creation, the heartbreak and the delight of God. All the noisy and the great works of man fall into silence before the wonder of a child.

When we bring them into the world, we take up the highest responsibility on earth—the guardianship of a human being. For children are not our possessions, to do with as we please. They do not exist for our convenience. They are not pretty toys to amuse us in our boredom, nor the rubber cement to hold together our marriages, nor yet the handy little servants to assist with the farm and house work. They do all these things, and many more; but that is not why they are here.

They belong, not to us, but to the human race. The law allows us to throw our crockery around, but not our children. This is not because they are so costly, or such works of art. It is because they are members of the human family, with all the rights and properties thereof. In this sense they are no less than we, the parents. And in this sense they do not belong to us, but to themselves.

Children are people. This is a point that we parents must get very straight, right from the beginning, if we are to understand our children as God understands them. Children are distinct human personalities. Theirs is the dignity of beings who later will have in their own hands the choosing of their life's direction and destiny.

They belong to themselves. Yet they do not belong to themselves. For ultimately the child belongs neither to his parents nor to himself but to his Creator. The human race is inescapably linked to Him who made it; and to Him the child will finally be responsible. To be born is to be forever within the area of God's concern and God's authority.

It becomes clear then that parents are more than just Mommy and Daddy. They are given the important position of a steward, "one who acts as a supervisor or administrator . . . for another."[2] God entrusts to us, for a time, that which is His.

When we understand the prior claim of God upon our children, our ideas about training them can begin to take definite shape. We discover a long-range goal. We find answers to many bothersome questions. We find the ability to love our children, not now with a selfish possessive love, but with a love mixed with respect, more deep and more sure.

Now the Bible has not a great deal to say directly concerning the bringing up of children—a few proverbs, a few injunctions in the New Testament. Yet actually the whole Bible is a book on how to raise children. Because the Bible is a record of how God handles people; and children are people. The ways of God with men are the perfect pattern for our training of our own children.

As we learn to know our own heavenly Father, the way opens up before us. As guardians we now begin to ask, not "What do I want my child to be?" but "What does the Father want my child to be?" How does He look upon the little ones? What is His mind concerning them? How would He like for us to handle them? The answers come as we learn to know Him.

Not that anyone will ever have all the answers, for none of us will ever fully comprehend either God or our child. But we can make progress. Perhaps the following ideas will do for a start.

GOD UNDERSTANDS CHILDREN

"But, Mommy, I don't *want* to go to heaven," my little boy told me earnestly. "I like it more better here!"

40

What should I have said to him? Should I have laughed at the cute remark? been horrified at such a wicked declaration? explained the glories of heaven? told him to run and play?

Whatever my reaction, I could be very sure that God understood the little fellow completely.

Many of the baffling things our children do are in reality part of a quite normal pattern of development. These growth patterns, as discussed by the best books on child growth, help us a good deal to know what to expect and what not to expect. For example, the mother whose four-year-old tells fanciful tales of his supposed exploits should know that children of that age cannot always distinguish between the real and the imaginary, and not be unduly alarmed.

We need to understand how children grow. We need to gain insight into children's needs, especially the deeper ones. A child has many needs. For one thing, he is a beginner. A child has a very great amount of growing up to do, and there are no short cuts. He will have to walk every inch of the way himself. He must discover the world he lives in, the kind of person he wishes to be, what God is all about. Columbus didn't have the exploring job ahead of him that every newborn does. Give the child room. He needs it.

He needs other things besides room to grow in. He needs security—a home base from which to carry out his explorations. It is as bad to be set adrift as to be confined. A child needs a refuge in Father and Mother, and later on in his heavenly Father. He needs to be sure of this refuge.

Our understanding is vital also in the area of specific religious instruction—about God, prayer, the Bible, giving. Here we are in particular danger of teaching rote patterns rather than making these matters real to the child. The understanding parent will endeavor to make all spiritual instruction relevant to the child, down on his level. After all, when God talks to us, He comes down to where *we* are.

Being a mother isn't something a woman can do with eyes shut; it demands her clearest sight. As one mother said, it takes no imagination to hit a child, but it takes all the creative

41

resources one possesses to train constructively. To be matter-of-fact, flexible, and positive in handling a child; to be firm or casual as occasion requires; to mix respect for the child as a being a little lower than the angels with the calm practicality required to steer him safely through a day: this takes our highest maturity. It takes the life of Christ in us.

GOD LOVES CHILDREN—DYNAMICALLY

It is as important that a child understand as that he be understood; that he give to life as that he take from it. God *understands;* but further, He *loves,* and loves purposefully.

To love is to become involved. It is to enter another's life, to rejoice with him, to weep with him, to bear his burdens and grieve over his sins, to keep the vision of what he can become.

Some of us, viewing our children's imperfections, have a deep-rooted feeling that it is our job to hastily polish them up into correct little beings whom God can accept. This is not so. God has already accepted our children, because when He came to Calvary He accepted the human race. There is no depth to which anyone can fall but that He has already been there. We can relax on this point. God already greatly loves our children. He is already involved.

I believe that God delights in the little ones. They are a masterpiece of His hand. All the fashions of Paris are not more beguiling than a lassie's blue eyes. A heaven of stars is not more mysterious than a boy's eager mind. No rose petals can caress like a child's soft hand; no satin is smoother than his cheek. We shop for expensive ornaments for our houses, and forget that they already contain earth's loveliest, dearest treasures. Symmetrical and graceful in shape, yet full of the fire of life, they are the art of God.

Lest anyone think otherwise, Christ gathered the children to Him and blessed them. He did more—He became a child.

God is always aware of each child. But a small child is not aware of God. He knows only the concrete surroundings of his little life. Much of his conception of what God is like will come from his parents and later from his church. The life he

42

knows at home will become the foundation of his responses to living, and to God.

Teaching a child to know Him is our primary objective as Christian parents. Now, some of us define Christian training too narrowly; we think of "doing our duty by the child" in terms of churchgoing, teaching prayers and verses, giving instruction on ethical matters, punishing infractions of rules. Much of this is training in religious exercises and moral disciplines.

But to teach a child what God is like, the thing we are really after, is a different matter. The base is much broader. It widens out to include not only the moral but all aspects of human life.

For God cannot be confined to the "religious" part of a person. If we give this impression, we set up a conflict between "spirituality" and the wholesome joys of living. The rebellious will choose the latter and shake off the apparently irksome controls of religion. The sincere, sensitive child may become very religious at the cost of stifling his natural and "worldly" impulses, squeezing the vigor of his life into a narrow rigid "spiritual" box, and becoming desperately unhappy.

God is in all of life. True, He is concerned primarily with winning the little one's love. But that love is the more easily won if a child sees that God is interested in all of him. A God who drenched the world in color and bothered to build crystal gems into dull rocks surely is interested in a child's sense of beauty. A God who gave the child a brain vastly more complex than any IBM machine surely is interested in his reaching after knowledge. All the thousand potentials of a child are from Him. No little segment or rut of a human personality can contain Him who made all that is made.

Christian training of children is a whole way of living. It has to do with a child's mental ability as well as his manners, with vaccinations as well as VBS, with *Peter Pan* as well as *Pilgrim's Progress,* with playing as well as praying, and rides on Dad's shoulder as well as rides to church. It has to do with picnics, report cards, diets, a youth's first love, a baby's first smile. It includes all of an earthly life bestowed on us as a valuable and blessed gift, as well as a heavenly life.

Christian parents can widen their children's horizons, and teach them the fullness of living, and encourage them in all constructive activities, and all the while be shaping their idea of God. Indeed, it must be so if the child is to respond to God with all his heart. He must respond to life before he can respond to the God who made life. If a child thinks of God in terms of a cramped, ascetic religiosity, he may submit to its demands out of fear. But if he sees God as the wise and purposeful Creator of a life that was designed to be gloriously full and upright, he can choose God with all the loves of his heart. And if he does not, he knows what he is doing.

THE WORLD IS GOD'S GIFT TO A CHILD: WE ARE GUARDIANS OF OUR CHILD'S AWARENESS

A child has a right to be happily acquainted with the splash of waves and the way earthworms wiggle. It's a wide, wide world, full of fascinating surprises, and it all belongs to him. He will taste, touch, poke, dump, smell, examine, and listen until he's stopped. Encourage him, within reasonable bounds. If he is digging a hole in the dirt, let him. Later on he'll do it with a package of seeds to plant, and be fascinated by the sprouting bean plants, and (remembering George Washington Carver and his peanuts) who knows what can come of that!

Parents need to share a little of this zest for life. It needn't always be fishing trips and picnics, though these are surely part of every family schedule. However, most parents are busy working most of the time. We need then to find the little ways to enjoy God's world. Mother can snatch a moment on the way to the clothesline to point out the billowy cloud that looks like an elephant. She can marvel with her youngster at the blooming redbud, or laugh at an ant running along with a huge crumb. Or feel the warm sunshine in the grass. It doesn't take much—a moment to look, listen, and wonder, and to say, "Look, dear—God made this."

When the child is older he extends his awareness of the world through reading, music, and other systematic study.

Perhaps the best way for parents to cultivate these interests is to enjoy them too! One of my precious childhood remembrances is the time my father took us older children into the car (for lack of other privacy) and read us *Tom Sawyer*. Good music in the home, books brought from the library or second-hand store and read aloud, trips to the zoo and museum and art gallery—there is no end to the way an alert parent can unlock the vast treasuries of the handiwork of God as discovered and put to use by men. In every direction, God has built into His world marvels and wonders.

Show your child that he may open his eyes and see.

A SELF IS GOD'S GIFT TO A CHILD: WE ARE GUARDIANS OF OUR CHILD'S POTENTIAL

The word "self" has come into much disfavor in some circles, as something to be ashamed of and destroyed for the sake of Christ. Behind this idea is an unfortunate confusion of terms. We recognize the physical body—no mistaking that; but the inner self (just as real) is, we feel, something to be suppressed. If we insist to our young people that they become "nothing," let's not be surprised if they turn out to be nothing! A self is a necessary thing, a gift from God. Remember, Christ came to us as a human personality. If a child is to give himself to God, he must have something to give!

What is wrong with man is the basically twisted *direction* he is going with that self—his egocentric outlook, his wrenching loose from his Creator. Now if a car is going the wrong way down a road, we don't need to wreck the engine and upholstery; we turn the car around. So with ourselves. We might say, there is the self of *equipment* and the self of *direction*. To serve Christ a young man needs the very same equipment—the same intelligence, will power, imagination, and emotional powers that he uses to live for himself. It is the basic change of direction that he needs, the giving of himself to Christ; then He comes in to redeem, and the young person starts out becoming the truly gracious and upright creature God designed him to be in the first place.

45

A child is equipped. He has talents—in music, mechanics, administration, writing, road building. A child's creativity in the areas of his ability needs to be encouraged. A recent article, "Your Child May Be More Gifted Than You Think," points out that the creative spark most children are born with is knocked out of them by fourth grade![3] Your youngster's talents can blossom instead of wither if you will give your honest attention to his creative efforts, commending them, pointing out a fault or two, giving him opportunity for good training. Once when we moved to a new house, my father said that we would buy a piano before we bought a dining room table. We did, too. In fact, there were two pianos—one in the parlor and an old fellow in the back bedroom, so that all four children currently taking lessons could practice every day.

Don't tell a child exactly how to do everything, like drawing a chicken in three adult strokes. The chickens he makes himself will be more satisfying to him and he may end up drawing a much better one than you ever could. Do join him occasionally in cutting, drawing, and hammering. Later on the teenager will continue to express himself aesthetically in the symmetrical way he builds a table or the young woman in the artistic way she chooses her clothes and decorates her home.

Then there are the everyday skills. Mother and Dad can be the world's best teachers in know-how around home. They can give each child personalized attention—a teacher's dream! Father and son can take up anything from radio to carpentry, and Father makes a wonderful driving instructor for his girls. My interest in sewing comes from my mother. She wouldn't put up with a sloppy joy, either.

Activity of these kinds makes idle time constructive. A boy who is practicing his violin or edging the lawn won't be hanging around the drugstore. He can't be building a generator and dragging main at the same time.

On the other hand, his schedule should not be nerve rackingly jammed. Young folks need time for themselves, to think the long, long thoughts of youth and to watch the grass grow.

To realize his potential, a child needs to learn to handle problems, to attack them courageously and solve them imaginatively. W. D. Ellis writes that a basic attitude of the successful people he knew was refusal to be licked by a problem.[4] Nancy of the comic strip is so appealing because she always finds a forthright way to solve her difficulty. If one straw is too short to reach the soda, hook it up with another. If glue won't work, try string. If you made a flop in orchestra, try the school paper.

A child who has all his problems solved for him will grow up flabby inside. If he runs away from problems when he is little, he will run away from them when he is big. Jenkin Lloyd Jones wrote, "These are not good years for bawlers, whiners, and hiders-in-the-closet."[5] Parents can help, both by allowing a young person to face difficulties as he is able, and by themselves being the kind of people who are not afraid to tackle things. For parent *and* child, calmness, objectivity, and constructive search for solutions go together. Just as anxiety, timidity, withdrawal, and giving up to problems go together. So, allow your child to undertake things, to experience victories and failures of his own. Teach your child to struggle.

Now it may sound as if all we need to do is put up the green light on the Road to Improvement, and our children will Go Go. Unfortunately, no. It takes a judicious mixture of firmness, patience, and not insisting on too much perfection to keep them at it. But it's worth it.

A word is in order about retarded and gifted children. In training a retarded or handicapped child, the emphasis is on abilities, not disabilities. Recognize his limitations, of course; but don't pity him into helplessness. Teach him to be as self-reliant as possible. It's marvelous what people minus fingers, arms, legs, and high IQ's have learned to do. And give that little retarded fellow a special dose of love in ways he understands.

Gifted children are often difficult. They don't want to do things the way they are told. However, instead of paring them down to average, let them put to work all they've got. They won't be happy otherwise. Be matter-of-fact about their

47

giftedness. A child who is constantly reminded that he is superior may mount a pedestal and lose communication with "inferior" people. He may wind up with a golden image of himself which he spends the rest of his life trying to live up to, feeling terribly superior when he does and terribly inferior when he doesn't, unable to live on the solid ground of his actual achievements and failures. I like to think of intellect as a tool. You don't go around feeling proud of a tool; you use it. What does it matter how the other fellow's compares? You've got yours, and you get to work with it. Nobody will ever exhaust God's possibilities anyway, even with the best mind in the world.

The odds and ends of knowledge, the skills your child picks up here and there, the ingenuity he develops will stand him in good stead all his life. These add to the inner resources and courage with which he faces life, and to his general helpfulness in the work of the Lord. Mental and physical laziness is no credit to a Christian. And the basis of many abilities, the attitude of overcoming, are laid in childhood.

Teach your child, that he may gird up his loins and do.

OTHER PEOPLE ARE GOD'S GIFT TO A CHILD: WE ARE GUARDIANS OF OUR CHILD'S RELATIONSHIPS

The growing child enters a world of people, and he needs to define his social attitudes. The basic one he needs to know, the one from which all others spring, is love; for "love is the fulfilling of the law." Parents cannot force a child to love: this is his own response. But parents are given to him by God as a picture book of what true love is like.

For this reason the harmony between mother and father is of extreme importance. Children sense well enough how parents feel toward each other. A Christian speaker gave this advice to husbands, "If you want to love your children more, love your wife more." The same goes for wives. Nobody can build a happy home on top of a volcano. Rifts between parents, quarrelings, and broken homes have sowed in countless children the seeds of rebellion, bitterness, misery, and gnawing insecurity, and obscured for them the face of God. Children need both parents. Children need parents who get along, not in an armed truce "for the sake of the kids," but in true God-given love.

So, if Father takes Mother out once in a while for the evening, and Mother speaks cheerfully to Father and gives him a child-viewed kiss, it's good for everybody. The child is unconsciously laying his own basis of happy marriage someday.

A vital aspect of love is that parents give of themselves—spelled TIME. Nothing, not the most glittering gift from Santa-Claus-land, can take the place of Mom reading stories to the little ones and Dad discussing his son's dating problems with him. What we value, we give our time to. Sometimes I think we feel obligated to everything else, from sewing circles to sales pitches, more than to our children. What doth it profit a man if he gain a whole extra section and lose his own child?

Time to talk with them. Time to play.

Ruth Clark sent questionnaires to 22 successful Christian families for their training secrets. One definite conclusion was, the family did things together.[6] I'll never forget how my dad helped us level out a flat place on a hillside for a badminton court, and then played badminton with us. And how one evening, after we children had spent the day making and delivering May baskets, there was a knock on the door; and there was Dad's May basket to us—a wastebasket piled full of old shoes and other funny things. Not that he was always with us, being in our way; but he had a knack for getting mixed up in our happy times.

A third aspect of love: be sure your child knows you love him even when he does wrong. One girl said, "My folks only like me when I am doing what they want me to do. But this past year I did something I shouldn't have done; and although I am sorry for it now, my parents can't forget it."[7] Forgiveness is the essence of redeeming love. Children need to be forgiven, and to know it. One small fellow, after a few rounds of bedtime discipline, snuggled up close and pressed his wee head against Daddy's breast, hard; he wanted to be quite sure Daddy still loved him.

49

A few practical suggestions to show love. *Tell* the child you love him. Pay prompt and cheerful attention to his needs, from diapering to doctoring. Give sympathetic attention (not cry-baby pity) to his hurts, failures, problems. Provide happy little surprises, as Grandma did when she took a thrilled little boy on a bus ride to town, just he and she. Resign from the Screaming Mothers' Club and maintain a pleasant, courteous tone of voice around the house. Give physical affection—kisses, caresses—as age and inclination warrant. And put him to bed happy! Always when you tuck him in, commend something he has done or suggest some fun coming tomorrow.

The child responds, learning to give back love. Encourage him. My sister talks animatedly to her tiny one as she handles him, eliciting smiles and coos. (I don't think she'd neglect a baby if she had ten years' ironing stacked up!) Enjoy the sticky kisses and bungling attempts to "help Mommy" while you may. Appreciate efforts to please you. One lively girl was often difficult; but at the end of a particular day, she burst into tears at bedtime and asked, "Wasn't I a *little* bit good today?" Mother hadn't bothered to notice.[8] Allan Sherman tells the story of a boy who heard Grandma say she needed a "football" for a party. He traded his new sled and all his marbles for an old football, and shined it up to give Grandma. Seeing it, his mother burst out laughing. "A *fruit bowl* is what Grandma wants," she said, "not a football." Later, jerking with sobs, the boy was called downstairs. There stood Grandma amid uncles and aunts, proudly displaying a huge fruit bowl, on top of a pile of fruits, his football. "From a child is beautiful, anything," she said.[9]

A child's world expands to include brothers and sisters (let's hope there are some). And cousins, uncles, neighbors, school friends, and all sorts of other people. Parents can now teach more definitely concerning love: courtesy, understanding, respect for the other fellow's rights, sharing, taking responsibility, forgiving. The child needs freedom and time to learn: there will be plenty of quarrels, bad feelings, hurts, withdrawals, and tears along the way. Our problems in social relations exist, in fact, as long as we do.

50

Whatever the difficulties involved, don't shrink your child's world of friends—widen it. Let him mix happily with children of other nationalities and faiths, with handicapped, poor or rich children, and with grownups for that matter.

Help where you can, guide where you can, interfere only if you must, encourage the shy child, restrain the very aggressive child. For your own part, be careful not to show partiality to your children, and pay special attention to jealousy if it comes up. Be realistic about other people, not blaming your child for things that aren't his fault, or them for what is your child's fault. In general speak well of others, especially in the child's hearing; your attitudes are catching.

Let him grow into the social world at God's speed—not too fast. A child will reach a happier, steadier maturity if he isn't rushed. Guard against the disastrous modern push into grade-school dating and teen-age marriage. An eleven-year-old who wants to use mascara and go steady should be told firmly that she is prettier the way she is and can begin definite dating, with controls, at age so-and-so (use your discretion).

If love is the ideal basic attitude for all social relationships, there is another attitude your child definitely must learn—simply because the world has torn loose from the law of love. That attitude is respect for authority. For parents first of all. Parents are not to provoke children to discouragement; but children are also to obey their parents. Children can't do everything they please. They are born without knowledge, and besides they have a will of their own and want to do all sorts of things that won't work. As Solomon realistically stated, foolishness is bound into the heart of a child. It's up to the parents therefore to stay in control. For every child who goes out of bounds, generally speaking, there's a parent who's letting him.

I remember three boys who came over to visit us; they were barely inside the door when two of them were banging frightfully on the piano and dinner gong, and the third was going through my cupboards looking for something to eat. They habitually stormed about so that adults could hardly carry on a conversation.

51

No girl should run her mother ragged buying her a Christmas present. Every girl should help cheerfully around the house without nagging or bribing. We do our children no favor by permitting them to degenerate into insolent, self-centered, unmanageable persons heedless of instruction. Joey needn't be allowed to fuss and pout when he can't have his way. I refuse to comply with my own son's otherwise reasonable request if he presents it in the form of a rude demand.

Pampering and over-permissiveness are just as harmful to the personality as their opposite extremes. A person who grows up thinking he is the center of the universe will be warped; because he *isn't* the center of the universe. God is.

Rather, true love will go to all lengths to help children become the best and the strongest people. This is God's way with us. It needs to be our way with our children.

The child must be taught those things that make for life: honest work, self-discipline, respect for the law of the land and for another's person and property, and many other things. If he is to be taught, he must learn to listen. Self-control and the ability to live constructively begin with obeying Mother and Father. And the child will respect parents who teach these things, just as he respects a schoolteacher who makes him study hard.

Win your child, that he may open his heart and grow.

GOD'S OWN REDEEMING LOVE IS HIS GIFT TO A CHILD: WE
ARE GUARDIANS OF OUR CHILD'S CHOICE-MAKING

Christian training can perhaps be resolved into this: we are providing our child with the wherewithal for making choices according to life's true issues.

We are not finally responsible for the choices he makes. But we can provide the best we know how, the ingredients of choice-making. These are two: concepts, and the ability to choose.

The greatest choice our child will ever make, the North Star we have been guiding toward, is his decision for God in Jesus Christ. The better a child knows what God is like, the more decisive his choice.

You may think, now at last we are getting to Christian training. Not at all. You have already painted, to a large extent, your child's picture of the face of God, by the kind of person you are and the way you handle the child. You tell him that God is love. Does he know what true love is like? You tell him God forgives sins. Does he know how it feels to be forgiven? You tell him God does not accept evil. Do you face up to your own wrongdoing? Or are you cutting out the ground from under him by indulging in a little dishonesty on the side, or claiming as your royal right that violent temper? All this time you have been conditioning your child to (or away from) love, forgiveness, right values.

Doctrines are useful to clarify thinking. But the choosing of Christ is not a matter of putting doctrines into our spiritual pockets. A turning to Christ is rooted in the deep choices of the heart. It is what we *are*, from our manners to our personal spiritual radiance, that our children lay up in their hearts. I have wonderful parents. My mother is one of those genuine people whose Christianity is not a front but a strength, and my father's cheery dedication made him beloved by everyone. I've forgotten most of what they said; my life was built by what they were.

The time comes, however, to crystallize by specific teaching the child's concepts of things spiritual. His idea of what God is like can now be made more systematic and definite. The person of Christ and His "Come unto me" become all-important. The child needs to learn what God has in mind for the human race in general, and for him in particular. He needs to understand the practicalities of the Holy Spirit in his life.

Sin needs to be defined—not as a jumble of inconsequential acts or the breaking of meaningless rules, but in the context of God's character, as the thwarting of God's gracious purposes for His whole creation. Evil must not become to the child a vague, looming, fearful threat filling the whole horizon, but a thing that comes in definite shapes, that can be recognized, overcome, forgiven. The child must learn to face definitely the unrighteousness within himself, not in hopeless guilt, but in realistic co-operation with God.

53

Parents can take the lead, by clear teaching and matter-of-fact applications. A definite advantage of home training is the *absence* of highly emotional pressures—we are apt to think through things better when we aren't being chased by over-wrought feelings. Home is a wonderful place to take the first steps of faith. Of the 97 children in the 22 families mentioned previously, 89 were led to the Saviour in their own homes, by their own parents.

Further instruction is available in church, Sunday school, Bible classes. This sort of regular teaching over the years is essential for an intelligent grasp of Bible truths. Christian institutions also make an appeal for the child's loyalties, to counter-balance the tremendous appeals from the world at large. Most of us are convinced enough of the value of our church program to take part in it regularly.

There is the vital area of a child's own personal studies, his private reading, his discussions with others about matters spiritual. For some children this is more significant than sermons; they like to work out things for themselves. Other children would rather learn by listening.

But always, they will have to carry home what they hear and put it to work in the realms of their own experiences, to choose, and choose, and choose again the way they will go. As their ideas about God, and sin, and what life is for, and what they themselves are like become more clear, they are able to go meaningfully about this business of making choices. As they understand who Jesus Christ is, they become able either to turn to Him in thankful receiving, or to shut Him out in unbelief (we earnestly pray they will not).

Concepts need to be made, then, and values straightened out. There is a second factor in a child's choice-making: his inner *ability* to choose; to make real decisions, right down where he lives. Babies, for example, cannot choose. Neither, really, can children who are driven by compulsions and fears, or children who have had all their decisions made for them to the point of paralysis of their own wills, or who are literally slaves to their own whims because they have never had to do anything they didn't want to. These persons are ill. They do choose, of course, the best they can; and God sees the smallest effort they try to make. But the compulsive person needs help to come back into daylight where he sees things normally, and the person who has had his way all his life needs to bump up hard against a few facts of life and a God who cannot be shoved around. The best choices are made, someone said, when nobody is pushing and nobody is pulling; when the child "owns himself" and consciously determines his actions.

I believe that strong church families need to be careful that children are not responding to pressure rather than to the still voice of God. We are sometimes more interested in conformity than growth. Parents who are trying to force their child into a rigid spiritual mold do not understand either what God is like or what children are like. One father created such bitterness in his son by relentlessly forcing him into family prayers on threat of punishment that it took the son many years to cross that barrier and come to Christ.

The huge auditorium was excessively hot, the sermon long. Everyone was uncomfortable in the stuffy air. Yet when a small child took off a shoe, the mother hastily and crossly forced it back on. Why? What was she afraid of if her little one, hot and uncomfortable, took off a shoe?

Why do parents insist that tiny tots sit and sit through long services, and object to nurseries and extended Sunday schools that would be far more meaningful to the children? Certainly children need to learn to sit still a moderate length of time; but they may as well be listening to something they can understand.

Why are even the young ones continually pressured to be saved and then baptized? It's one thing to keep the way open, and another to push. A child who responds now to social pressures will have to work his own way through later anyway, with added difficulty. We can trust God to work with the child, at His own speed.

Why are a teen-ager's questions about the existence of God and the validity of certain rules crushed down with the blank statement: It's a sin to doubt, to question? Can truth not stand without our protection?

55

Why do we try so hard to force children into set patterns of prayer, speech, conversion—patterns that may not be working too well even for adults?

One wonders at times whether the parent is concerned so much with the child's growth as with his own reputation as a "spiritual" parent. If he is afraid of what other people will think, he will be threatened by his child's lapses and be needlessly strict and unkind. Or he may feel that God is demanding this rigid attitude, that God Himself feels that way toward children. Parents who feel themselves in the hands of a stern, demanding, punitive Judge will tend to be that way themselves. Love gives way to fear; relaxation to tension; peacefulness to anxiety; understanding to relentless demand; inward growth to outward conformity. Here the *parent* needs to find out what God is like.

Whatever the cause, it is possible not so much to *expose* a child to God's values as to *impose* a thick shell of conformity. The behavior our child adopts, the actions he performs at our insistence—these do not necessarily express the true directions of his heart. For much as we would like to, we cannot actually change a child's heart: only God can do that. For this reason our goal is the child's own response to God.

It is not conformity, therefore, but genuine choice that makes a dynamic Christian.

A child needs to exercise his choice-making muscles. He starts in easy but early: what socks to wear, which friend to visit. Problems get harder: whether to join Scouts or take up a paper route. The big ones are ahead: what vocation to choose, whom to marry. A wise parent will neither dictate nor ignore, but will provide the right balance of freedom and protection from situations too big for the child.

The moral area is more difficult than others. One cannot allow his child to wander into lawless deeds—there are too many consequences, and sin tends to enslave. Probably a younger child should have freedom to talk rather than act. When a small boy said, "I don't like to go to Sunday school!" a wise man replied, "It's all right for you to tell me that— but you're going." Children need to be free to discuss, question, oppose points of view on matters that concern them. Later, they will begin to guide some actions by their own views of right and wrong (they won't always choose well, or see eye to eye with their parents). The time comes when they are on their own.

As the child is ready, he responds to his Saviour. It is his decision, not ours. Ours is to show him the redeeming grace of God in Jesus Christ, and to watch and pray.

If our child chooses ill, or becomes wayward, we cannot approve. But we need not be unduly shocked. As Eugenia Price puts it, "human nature is human nature and we all have it."[10] We cannot become judgmental, because of the motes and the beams in our own eyes. He only that is without sin dares cast the uncompassionate stones. No, we remain open to them, watching from the housetop and running to them when they return repentant. If they do not return, we grieve, but with hope; for God Himself has taken the final responsibility of wooing by His Spirit the heart of a man.

Nor need we blame ourselves for everything. We will never train a child perfectly. This is part of the stress of life. Also, our child's world includes not only his home but his school, church, friends, a particular culture, a particular age. Myriads of forces are at work upon him.

When our children choose well, we rejoice. When they rise up to oppose the world's creeping stain with God's purity, and the world's dishonesties with God's truth, and the world's hatreds with the Saviour's love, we rejoice, and the angels with us.

This is our reward, that we have shepherded our child safely into life. For we cannot keep him forever, except in our hearts and prayers. He will not always live where we live nor think exactly as we think. We would not want it. This is what we have been striving for always—to bring our child into his own maturity.

Our rejoicing and hope is this, that when our darling leaves home, he is simply entrusted more completely than ever into the heavenly Father's care. For no matter how well we love our child, God loves him more. If we made mistakes, God makes none. If we misunderstood, God understands. If we were willing to sacrifice, to give our heart's best, He more. He proved all this when He gave His own, His only Son. He can overrule all failures, answer all prayers, cause all things to work together for good to them that love Him.

The guardianship is over. The child is now responsible to Him who made him. When he was born into the world, he entered the area of God's concern. He is in it still.

Release your child, that he may go forth and live.

About the Writer

Phyllis Martens (Mrs. Elmer) was born in Mountain Lake, Minnesota. A year later she sailed to India with her missionary parents and spent ten years of her childhood there, the oldest of eight children—seven girls and a boy. She received the B.A. degree from Tabor College in Hillsboro, Kansas, and the M.A. in English from Kansas University. For six years she taught English and related subjects in Pacific College, Fresno, California. Her husband, Elmer A. Martens, is pastor of the Butler Avenue Mennonite Brethren Church of Fresno, where they live with three small children. She is much interested in the field of personality as it relates to Christian teaching and as it concerns the raising of children.

FOOTNOTES

1. Louis Untermeyer in *Modern American and British Poetry*, edited by Untermeyer (Harcourt, Brace and Co., 1935), p. 196.
2. *World Dictionary*.
3. John Kord Lagemann, "Your Child May Be More Gifted Than You Think," *Reader's Digest* (May, 1963), p. 246.
4. William D. Ellis, "Make Way for the No-Problem Guy," *Reader's Digest* (May, 1963), p. 95 ff.
5. Jenkin Lloyd Jones, "Teach Your Child to 'Love the Storm,'" *Reader's Digest* (February, 1963), p. 127.
6. Ruth C. Clark, "Homes That Make Christians," *Moody Monthly* (April, 1960), p. 26 f.

7. Told by Clyde M. Narramore, "Psychology for Living," Booklet No. 33—"The Kind of Parents Young People and Children Want," p. 4.
8. Told by Fulton Oursler, "There Is Magic in a Word of Praise," *Reader's Digest* (originally printed August, 1951).
9. Allan Sherman, "A Football for Grandma," *Reader's Digest* (February, 1960).
10. Eugenia Price, *Woman to Woman* (Grand Rapids, Mich.: Zondervan Publishing House, 1959), p. 203.

Chief Books Used

Frances Ilg and Louise Bates Ames, *Child Behavior*. New York: Harper and Brothers, 1955.

Margaret Bailey Jacobsen, *The Child in the Christian Home*. Wheaton, Ill.: Scripture Press, 1959.

Benjamin Spock, *Problems of Parents*. Boston: Houghton Mifflin Company, 1962.

AMERICANS *of our generation have experienced a greater advance in their material standard of living and a more pervasive change in their way of life than occurred in all the previous centuries of Western history.*

—Carl Kreider, in Stewardship in an Economy of Abundance.

4

STEWARDSHIP OF OUR POSSESSIONS

ALTA MAE ERB

THE Christianizing of her possessions is a great task that confronts the Christian woman in this twentieth century.

Scan any current periodical with many advertisements. The great majority of the ads are planned to catch the eyes and hearts of women. This assumes that the woman is the prime influence in securing the family's possessions. It is she who senses the need for the many items, such as furniture, utensils, energy-saving devices, foods, clothes (for most of the family perhaps), and paraphernalia for leisure hours.

It is the woman who cares for all these possessions. The Christian woman has a deep sense of responsibility for the nurture of the bodies, souls, and spirits of her family. She works continually in the midst of things. A great danger of being mastered by things threatens her.

GOD'S OWNERSHIP

"Behold, the heaven and the heaven of heavens is the Lord's . . . the earth also, with all that therein is" (Deuteronomy 10:14).

"For every beast of the forest is mine, and the cattle upon a thousand hills" (Psalm 50:10).

"The silver is mine, and the gold is mine" (Haggai 2:8).

When God led Israel into the Promised Land, He made it very emphatic that "the land is mine." God may say "mine." He owns all things on the basis of creation alone.

61

The house with its furnishings for comfortable living, the utensils a woman uses to prepare food for the family, the family yard and garden, the shelves of books, and the woman herself with her feminine desires are a part of the "all that therein is."

The created things of the universe have no value apart from the use they may be to some being. So God created man and woman and loaded them with benefits. Psalm 68:19.

"Being all-sufficient unto Himself in His infinite attributes, He nevertheless counts it His chief glory to graciously administer the inexhaustive resources of His material empire for the benefit of His peopled world."[1]

God created grass and herbs and trees. The green herbs were prepared to be food for man and animals. The animals were prepared for our food, our clothing, our power. The lodes of minerals He put in the earth give us heat and power. God told man to subdue the earth and have dominion over every living thing. All things were made for us.

However, God warned Israel that when they came from the manna diet to the fruit, oil, honey, and abundance of meat, they must be careful not to forget whose power and might gives them all this rich living. Deuteronomy 8:11-13, 17, 18.

I may overestimate my own power to make a fitting and attractive garment. God wants us to keep aware of who designed the cloth, who prepared the dyes, from what created materials the cloth was made, who made the machines that turn out yards of goods so expertly, who discovered this manufacturing process, and who revealed the idea to them. Trace each gift back to God, who has given every natural product and every power that uses them.

Woman was certainly in the thought of God when He shaped many different flowers, when He colored the clays of certain areas of land, when He made the visible spark in the lightning for a man to discover, when He created the flaxen plant with its seed. God was and is more desirous to give women things for their happiness than is any mother to give her children gifts for their pleasure. God has made a host of material things available to satisfy the human wants of a woman. Since He made the woman, He also knew her needs.

The things God created are not evil. "God saw every thing that he had made, and, behold, it was very good" (Genesis 1:31). The Christian believes God has given us all things richly to enjoy. I Timothy 6:17. We pray, "Give us this day our daily bread." In this we recognize that soils, harvesters, mills, yeast, heat, and bakeries are all from God, under His control. Man outside of Christ may make products from God's plants to ruin bodies or he may release atomic energy to destroy his fellow man. But the Christian woman need not look upon any of God's creation as evil in itself if she believes in God as creator of all things. Things are not bad, but she can put them to bad uses.

To deny oneself the use of things is not necessarily Christian. Paul calls asceticism "will worship" (Colossians 2:23). To use God's gifts in a proper way and with thankfulness is the right and privilege of God's people.

God also owns the Christian woman by a special right—the right of redemption. If a woman be in Christ, she is a new creature: "old things are passed away; behold, all things are become new. And all things are of God" (II Corinthians 5:17, 18). This new woman has nothing that she did not receive. The lordship of Christ means that Christ is Lord of all or not Lord at all.

Count your blessings from God as you keep house, in each room of the house. Count them when you share your house with guests; when you replace a deteriorated possession with a new one, perhaps a better kind; when your child leaves the house for school; when the family goes to church; when you shop at a supermarket, and when you sit to read, and meditate and praise.

"Our concept of God as the Creator determines the degree of our recognition of Him as the sole owner of His entire creation, and His right to delegate, designate, and direct the use of His possessions, according to His purposes which are built upon the eternal foundation of His love."[2]

The growth of the kingdom in the Christian woman depends

on her relating the things of heaven to the things of earth.

O God, Thou the great Creator, remind us daily of Thy goodness to us in giving us rich gifts, physical and spiritual; but keep us very conscious that these things and powers all belong to Thee. May we appreciate them as from Thy hand.

OUR STEWARDSHIP

We give Thee but Thine own,
Whate'er the gift may be;
All that we have is Thine alone,
A trust, O Lord, from Thee.
—W. Walsham How, *Church Hymnal*.

"As each has received a gift, employ it for one another, as good stewards of God's varied grace" (I Peter 4:10, RSV).

THE CHRISTIAN WOMAN—A STEWARD

When the Holy Spirit came upon the disciples (men and women) at Pentecost, each said that nought of the things which he possessed was his or her own. This responsive attitude was a stewardship expression. Pentecost experience made it real to them that God owned everything. They accepted the divine principle and shared their possessions. Later the church lost much of this emphasis. The abundance of things in our day requires that we rethink the implications of God's ownership and our stewardship. The right relation to things rests upon our right relation to God.

Many of God's created things and powers are held by the woman as a steward for Him. Her possessions are a trust. She can say "my house" if she means mine to use for God's honor. The many large and small things which a woman must oversee speak of the importance of her stewardship.

The word "steward" originally was "stiward," or "keeper of the pen." From this lowly origin as the keeper of the livestock, the steward gradually rose to be the caretaker of any property. One time David the First, King of Scotland, turned over some land that had been forfeited to the crown to Walter Fitzfald, a trusted servant of the court. The king gave Fitzfald

64

the title of "Steward of Scotland." From that title the royal line of the Stuarts came. Ralph W. Sockman, in commenting on this, said: "This bit of history may serve to symbolize the possibilities of stewardship. To take the things that are lowly, things even of the sty, which can make men greedy and hog-like, and to lift them into royal usage, to send them forth to serve our fellow man . . . this is the art of Christlike owner-ship."[3]

THE CHRISTIAN WOMAN—A PARTNER WITH GOD

We are laborers together with God. Christ does not even call us servants but friends. God reveals to us, through Christ, His will for our stewardship. This is partnership. We are made in the image of God, fitted to work for His glory. Paul calls this "stewards of the mysteries of God." It really is a mystery to the non-Christian woman how any woman can live with all her things, with God as her reference for using them.

Each woman is a partner with God in running her home. God owns all that is found in the house. The housekeeper is the manager for God. We do not call the house furnishings secular and the housekeeping sacred. All things when used for God have a spiritual significance and are sacred. The woman's motive in keeping the house clean, in selecting furnishings, in buying food at the mart, in deciding on the line between necessity and luxury, is very important. She is working with God, making a good home for her family and friends.

Her many possessions are held as a trust from God, as a loan to her. Her housekeeping is a practical expression of her experience with God. All problems arising in the handling of her things for the best good of all concerned may be referred to God. Any possession not completely surrendered for the Master's use will always be a thorn in her flesh. "What value does this redecoration of our house have? It is beautiful. But does this beauty make me more beautiful within? Poor Mrs. —————— does need new wallpaper, but did we? How happy she would be with cheerful, clean walls. Maybe I should turn my eyes from beholding vanities. It seems to be all our guests see when they visit us. Now Jennie is nagging Fred to redecorate their house. . . . Some women don't care for beautiful things, but I do." And so the pricking may continue if God was not considered in some house project.

The Scriptures do not idolize poverty nor do they deny us the possession of things. Unfaithfulness in the use of possessions is what Jesus condemned. Matthew 25:14-30; Luke 16:10-13. A comfortable chair is not evil, but the steward must face the purpose in purchasing this chair. Is it right for me to buy another dress? Couldn't we have steak just this once? The genuineness of the need gives the answer. The answers are not easy. In considering what possessions are necessary for Christian living, we must consider what the woman herself must have for her best development and also what she must have for her service to others.

POSSESSIONS FOR SELF-DEVELOPMENT

"Lay not up for yourselves treasures . . . but lay up for yourselves treasures . . ." (Matthew 6:19, 20). Laying up treasures is not condemned. The same treasure might be earthly or heavenly. The owner determines this. Surely it is legitimate to acquire conveniences in the home if they really make one more useful in the kingdom. Our possessions are for more than mere existence. They are for life, for a full life.

"To live we must have freedom to realize ourselves. Some degree of liberty must be ours for individual action. We must be able to make plans; to arrange life in accordance with them; to choose; to have reasonable expectation as to the result of the choice. For all of which we must have control over some things. These things we must be absolutely able to count on; no one must have the power to take them from us."[4]

"There is no end to a woman's wants." This is true. Let any critic consider the many possible areas of need in managing a household. The Christian woman has a keen sense of responsibility for the best care, the best nurture, the fullest education for all facets of the personalities of the family. There is really no end to useful tools the homemaker can use.

However, not all women need the same kind or number of tools, in spite of what the advertisers may say. Personally I don't have an electric beater. I have little need for one. But my daughter may use hers daily. Different tastes, concerning which one should not argue, call for different things and also ask for different amounts of things. I often see in other women's living rooms embroideries I feel no need for. A guest at my house may not appreciate a decorative item that I have. Each woman comes out of a specific cultural background, from which she inherits certain patterns of interests.

Necessity is a relative term. As Christians each should own that which has value for her as she lives her own life with God. Right or wrong in possessions can never be judged by comparing possessions. Many women want to possess things like those most women have, or they desire the latest in household conveniences. Conformity is not Christian. We do not own for possessing's sake, but to do our best as God's stewards. Releasing time for the Lord's needed work is one Christian guide rule. Selfishness the Gospel rebukes. As we keep close to God, and then only, do we have the insight necessary to check our motives for adding possessions.

Luxury is also a relative term. Each woman must be very sensitive as to what is mere luxury and refrain from such possessions. The temptations are great. Someone may think that another has too fine a Bible, too good a carpet, china that is too costly, drapes that are too lovely, too many cupboards, too many books, too many African violets, too much rich food, too expensive a car, too costly a hobby, too big a house, too costly a vacation. It is difficult to judge rightly concerning one's own desires for luxuries. If we are fully dedicated to God, He can turn our eyes from beholding vanity, from the lust of the flesh and the pride of life. Surely luxury which we recognize to be such must be classed as worldliness.

POSSESSIONS FOR SERVICE TO OTHERS

Our possessions must "speak in accents of Saviourhood. He (God) wants property to articulate the Personality at the heart of the universe. Some property is already utilized to do this in whole or in part. If hospitals, churches, schools, and homes voice God, property everywhere must come to proclaim Him. The trustee of God's good will not be content to hear God only in moments of meditation. His God cannot be 'cribbed, cabined, and confined' to thought; He invades all of life. You cannot sever His from Him. The steward seeks to show God forth in the face of property. Or, to put it in other words, he has the conviction that property ought to do what God wants done. . . . Property is God's; stewardship is the means of exalting Him through it."[5]

"None of us liveth to himself" (Romans 14:7). "Whoso hath this world's good, and seeth his brother have need, and shutteth up his bowels of compassion from him, how dwelleth the love of God in him" (I John 3:17)? This question we need to hear often.

The rich man whose ground yielded abundantly was a "fool" because he thought he could be "merry" by himself. Luke 12:16-21. He laid up treasure for himself, but he lost it all. The rich young ruler wanted to keep his treasures from the poor. He did this but, no doubt, lost his soul. God knows the dangers in things; especially in many things. We become more selfish as things increase. We become more insensitive to the needs of others.

John Wesley said, "Get all you can, save all you can, give all you can." Jesus said, "The poor always ye have with you" (John 12:8). There can be no ownership apart from obligation to others.

BE THRIFTY

The 12 basketfuls gathered after the 5,000 had eaten are a strong hint against wastefulness. Too many dresses will certainly make me careless in caring for any one. Abundance of food does not encourage saving leftovers.

Appreciation of the wear that a carpet or a chair or a machine will receive will direct the buyer to look for good quality in the article. It is not necessarily Christian to buy cheap things. However, too fine a carpet may not be Christian either, for it may be too great an investment for floor covering when

68

the real necessities of other people are lacking to them. And it may not belong to the simple, unadorned life. Poor or good as a possession may be, we are bound to preserve its usefulness as long as possible. Christians mend clothes and furniture, and prevention of soiling is a part of thrift.

Long ago Herbert Hoover estimated that the United States spent a million dollars a day in superfluous eating in hotels and restaurants. What would be the figure today?

The woman who is mindful to take care of her possessions will also take care of public property, church property, the highways, the books in the public library, and the equipment in parks and roadside rest areas.

"[She] that is slothful in . . . [her] work is . . . [sister] to . . . [her] that is a great waster" (Proverbs 18:9).

The stewardship of keeping the family's possessions has been committed to woman. It is required in her that she be found faithful.

God, Thou who art intensely interested in Thy women stewards, keep us very sensitive to the right use of possessions, and give us help to be faithful and efficient stewards.

BEWARE OF COVETOUSNESS

Covetousness is usually defined as an inordinate desire and longing to possess that which is the right of another.

"Thou shalt not covet." God gave this command. Covetousness, therefore, is a sin. Paul classifies it with fornication, idolatry, uncleanness, unrighteousness, maliciousness, murder, and other gross sins.

"It is impossible to find any comprehensive definition of covetousness. Definitions can help, but cannot go to the root of the peril. To say that covetousness is 'inordinate desire,' or that a covetous person is 'avaricious,' 'greedy,' or 'mercenary' is hardly to define adequately. All these definitions must be further explained. For our purposes it may be enough to declare that covetousness is the *archenemy of Jesus' philosophy of stewardship*. It makes self the center and circumference of the universe; it is the negation of everything that stewardship stands for. It creates a selfish cruel world."[6]

69

All things are of God and God wants us to have possessions to use, but our liberty to control things must never turn into license. "Things are in the saddle, and ride mankind," said Emerson. And they ride with cruel spurs.

The covetous woman wants a new dress for a certain occasion, whether she needs it or not. Since her friend has a new stove, she must have one too, lest her friend's house become more attractive than her own. And she will be tempted at least to get the latest style vacuum cleaner before her neighbor does. Her wants may exceed her husband's income. She does not hesitate to make debts. Her desire may be so strong that she drives her husband to dishonesty. If her wants are met, her soul will be poisoned. Covetousness is a very insidious sin. It brings much unhappiness and discord.

Covetousness ignores God's claim of ownership. To know and think that I am God-owned and all that I have belongs to God counteracts covetousness. Jesus said we should not be anxious about food, drink, and clothes. We are of more value than birds, for which God cares. He will care for us. Seek the kingdom of God and His righteousness. Matthew 6:25-33. Give of yourselves to serving others; keep the body under the spirit's control. Deny to yourself ungodly acquisitions. Share your possessions. Consider the poor. Experience the joy of simple living. These are Christian antidotes.

When self-realization becomes self-aggrandizement is difficult to discern, even in one's self. But things soon sate the soul, and we need to "take heed, and beware." Remember the rich "fool." Remember Lot's wife. Blindness to the needs of others is one sure danger sign. Love of the indwelling Christ can cure covetousness.

Women like to collect a supply of things. It has always been thought that this was a God-given instinct. One lady said she wouldn't be caught in another depression in which she couldn't buy sheets. She had stored up sheets for many years. Was this God's directive? Won't God's ownership claim sanctify the collective instinct?

Apart from the grace of God, it is impossible for a woman to have great possessions and put God first in her life. Luke

18:18-30. Outside of Christ many possessions may dwarf the soul. Cares of this world, the deceitfulness of great possessions, and lust for things choke what God says to us and the Word becomes unfruitful in us. We need to "take heed and beware."

What doth it profit a woman if she gain the whole world and lose her own soul?

Holy God, search our hearts for any unholy love for things. Convict us deeply of the sin of covetousness and deliver us for the sake of Thy honor.

IN THE MIDST OF ABUNDANCE[7]

The woman of the world glories in the many available possessions in this day. The Christian woman fears lest she fail to discern the relation of the abundance to the "abundant." God has declared that a woman's life consisteth not in the abundance of things which she possesseth. Luke 12:15. Christ said that He came that a woman might have life, the more abundant life. John 10:10. But this abundant life does not derive from material objects. It often flourishes in the midst of poverty.

> The world is too much with us;
> Late and soon, getting and spending,
> We lay waste our powers.
> —Wordsworth.

A Christian woman needs to become keenly conscious and keep aware of the fact that a Christian lives in the world but is not of the world. We are glad for the many manufactured products business is preparing to ease the woman's life, to release much energy for the higher living. But we must see the snare. The manufacturer makes products for us, but he also manufactures tastes and demands. Clothing, furniture, dishes, and what not are planned to become obsolete quickly. Styles must change or the big business market would become glutted. Changing the color of phones sold thousands of

71

phones to no-new-phone-needers. A woman with a liking for red can find any kitchen item to meet this color taste. And more red kitchen items will be on the market tomorrow to tempt the woman. This color may sate the owner sooner or later. Will she then change to yellow?

We as Christian women must live in this economy of abundance with all its pressures and limited alternatives. Our life must be realistic. We have to conform in some respects. Sanitary regulations require indoor plumbing. A car is practically a necessity for suburb living.

Yet we know that God draws lines between worldliness and Christianity. His limitations we must seek that we may be saved from mere conformity. We experience often that it is difficult to balance budgets, but is it not more difficult to balance our desires, our ambitions, and our greeds? God has spoken, and we know by experience that it is true, "He [and she] that loveth silver shall not be satisfied with silver; nor he [and she] that loveth abundance with increase: this is also vanity" (Ecclesiastes 5:10).

In our economy what we know to be right values are colored so easily by the surrounding culture. Perhaps without being aware of it, I am succumbing to the power of high advertising and am taking unto myself things that I should not have. I think—they are good; I can have them; I can pay cash for them. But are they good for my soul, for my example in the church, for my heavenly security, for my service in the church and community?

Unless I keep very conscious in mind and heart of God's ownership and my stewardship under Him, I "will inevitably accept the standards and evaluations of those with whom I interact at an intimate level."[8]

"Drip dry"—can't I get one of those? Do I look "dressed" to my friends without some jewelry? My overshoes function well, but they are not shaped with heels. They must look funny. Shouldn't I give a little more time to arranging my hair? Such little, yet subtle dress questions may come to us as we live with women who have different standards.

In this day when building materials are easily obtained, we

can afford them, and we reconstruct our houses or build new ones. But does the expenditure change the efficiency of our Christian fellowship in the home? The values of our worldly environment dictate to us in big and small things far beyond our recognition. Only the soul honest before self and God can decide whether a modern convenience releases energy and time for noble uses or whether it is in answer to the lust of the eye.

Abundance of possessions creates insensitivity, because the more I have the more I want. And so I sense less than ever the needs of others. I become callous to the "forty-five per cent of American families who still have incomes of less than $4,000 annually, regarded as below reasonable necessary standards of living. Fifteen per cent of our families live on less than $2,000 per year—a level which must be regarded as poverty."[9]

"Abundance is not simply higher levels of income or more cars, refrigerators, and roast beef. It is the whole interdependent structure and process, and the value orientations and personal qualities and interests that are generated. One can't have the product without the whole process of production and its ordering of human relations. In short, stewardship is concerned with nothing less than man's responsibility to God as he participates in the whole technological-industrial-distributional system of his environing context, for stewardship is the active recognition of God over His whole creation; over the creative and productive processes in which men share, and the uses to which they put all the resources and means that come under their care and control."[10]

Christian ownership of possessions touches the human experience of women at very many points. Its practice is our challenge.

God, Thou who hast redeemed us, help us to live for Thee in the ungodly emphases of this present economy of abundance. We would be good stewards. Please take away our love for the world by giving us more love for Thee. Amen.

73

About the Writer

Alta Mae Erb is the wife of Paul Erb and the mother of Mrs. Winifred Paul, Scottdale, Pennsylvania, and Missionary J. Delbert Erb, Bragado, Argentina. She has eight grandchildren. The Erbs live in a third-floor apartment in the building of the Mennonite Publishing House, Scottdale, Pennsylvania, where they have both been employed for a number of years. Earlier Mrs. Erb taught at Hesston College and Goshen College for over 30 years. She has served the church she loves as minister's wife, church school teacher, writer, and speaker.

FOOTNOTES

1. Ralph S. Cushman, *The Message of Stewardship* (Abingdon Press, 1922), p. 37.
2. Virginia Ely, *Stewardship: Witnessing for Christ* (Revell, 1962), p. 44.
3. Charles M. Crowe, *Stewardship Sermons* (Abingdon, 1960), p. 105 f.
4. John M. Versteeg, *The Deeper Meaning of Stewardship* (Abingdon, 1923), p. 107.
5. *Ibid.,* p. 95 f.
6. Ralph S. Cushman, *op. cit.,* p. 134.
7. For many of the thoughts of this section, the author is indebted to A. T. Rasmussen in *Stewardship in Contemporary Theology.*
8. T. K. Thompson (Ed.), *Stewardship in Contemporary Theology,* "Stewardship in an Economy of Abundance," by Albert Terrill Rasmussen (Association Press, 1960), p. 231 f.
9. *Ibid.,* p. 246.
10. *Ibid.,* p. 231 f.

MAN's *earthly task is to realize his creat-*
ed uniqueness. As a Hasidic rabbi called
Zusya put it on his deathbed: "In the
world to come they will not ask me,
'Why were you not Moses?' They will
ask me, 'Why were you not Zusya?'"
— *Martin Buber, in Time.*

MAKING LIFE WORTH WHILE

Every soul that touches yours—
Be it the slightest contact—
Gets therefrom some good;
Some little grace; one kindly thought;
One aspiration yet unfelt;
One bit of courage
For the darkening sky;
One gleam of faith
To brave the thickening ills of life;
One glimpse of brighter skies—
To make this life worth while
And heaven a surer heritage.
— *George Eliot, 1819-80.*

5

STEWARDSHIP OF PERSONALITY

ELIZABETH A. SHOWALTER

PERSONALITY is a potent thing. It is like a perfume. A spoken phrase, a look, an action or reaction, a gesture—any of these can reach a long way in memory or in influence. A most stimulating book could be written on "Bouquet of Saints," in which the essence of well-lived lives would be distilled into a few pages for each. The Bible does it. Consider Esther or Ruth.

A few paragraphs can capture the fragrance of a life and dispense it for centuries. Sarah? Beautiful, gay, yet modest and obedient to her husband. Deborah? Wise, efficient, brave, able to send forth an army and its captain for the honor of the Lord. Elisabeth? Trusting, patient, devoted, undismayed. Priscilla? Apt to teach, alert to opportunity. Even a sentence is enough: Cornelia is remembered for her, "These are my jewels."

Perennial inspiration flows from II Corinthians 2:14:

> But to God be the thanks
> who in Christ ever leads us
> in His triumphal procession,
> displaying everywhere through us the sweetness
> of the knowledge of Him.
> For we are a fragrance of Christ.

This is Weymouth's rendering. Equally provocative of thought is Phillips' paraphrase:

> Thanks be to God who leads us,
> wherever we are,

>   on his own triumphant way
>   and makes our knowledge of him
>   spread throughout the world
>   like a lovely perfume!

The diffusion of this aroma is not a matter only of time, but of distance as well. I think of my friend the farthest from me and instantly there comes to my mind an image, a distinctive flavor, a whiff of her personality. It is sobering to think that the same is happening wherever I am known. It is almost overwhelming to think that over the globe we are intensifying or adulterating that composite image, or savor, or aroma that the word "Christian" gives to the other peoples of the world. This is one of the subtilities of our stewardship.

Personality is a window through which the light of God shines into the world. Each light is colored by the racial, family, and personal experience which has shaped the individual's life. Through Rahab shone faith. Through Mary devotion. Through Dorcas lowly, but loving, service. Without doubt some measure of all these virtues was found in each. But the peculiar contribution of these, and ten thousand times ten thousand more, is necessary to show all the grace and beauty of the Lord. Somewhere there is a place for our own special part of the whole that cannot be duplicated or initiated; likewise without the other parts there can be no whole. The Master Craftsman, who planned a crimson circlet for Mary's bodice and a golden circlet for the Infant's halo, gave to each its shape and hue. Take away either or exchange the two and the window becomes a distraction.

GOD'S PLAN FOR A WONDROUS BEING

The person is the root and source of stewardship, for when man was given personality, responsibility began. The waste and void became order and reality without choice. The oceans and the dry land, the grass, the sun, moon, and stars were called into being to fulfill their purpose by merely existing and obeying fixed laws. The creeping things and animals moved higher into realms of instinct. But as the chorus in the *Creation* repeats: "There wanted yet a wondrous being."

This need of God for response intrigues me. The inanimate could display His power; only a soul could display His personality. Almost every day the scientists ask us to stretch our concepts of time and space, of potentiality and possibility still farther as if we were not already paralyzed by the ultra-telescopic on the one hand and the infra-microscopic on the other. All this should call us, I think, to higher and higher concepts of the reality behind the façade of the material and to deeper and deeper surrender to the spiritual, which is reality at work within us. Our widening intellectual response to scientific discovery should be matched by a widening spiritual response to the testimony of the Scripture, of Christian saints of the ages, and of those of our day who dare push out our spiritual boundaries. To say it another way, the power that set the stars in their courses in such flawless harmony that the "morning stars sang together" also blew the breath of His Spirit into man, raising him from a clod to a being with spiritual potentiality. The power which raised Jesus from the dead now seeks to quicken our spirits. The power that brought forth water from the rock, and made a dry track through the sea, offers to make our deserts into gardens, our swamps into fruitful fields.

Jesus said that if the children were stopped from praising Him, the stones would cry out. I keep thinking about certain stones we see in exhibits and in museums. Under ordinary light they look like any stone you might pick up in a field; when ultraviolet light is turned upon them, they glow like jewels. The few stones which have this quality can be detected only by their response to this light. What a parable! No personality can become its utmost unless it responds to God: none can respond unless it is exposed. So we are stewardesses of our own response and of the possibility of response for our fellow men within the circle of our influence.

Here we are, each a unique personality, bearing within us the racial, the family, the personal characteristics that have focused to make us what we are. We carry also, within our subconscious, the physically and emotionally accumulated record of everything that has shaped us from the moment of conception. Of many of these factors we are fully aware. Of

79

others we are totally unaware. Naturally, we have not chosen any of our inherited characteristics and a scanty few of our environmental ones. While it is true we have deliberately cultivated some facets of our personalities and repressed others, we have often done this for expediency or because of social pressure, and even more often for reasons arising from our unconscious.

I remember, as a child, wondering why I did the unapproved acts my family seemed to hold me responsible for; my actions seemed to just happen that way. Not many years ago, when I awoke from a light anesthesia crying like an infant in my grown-up voice, I experienced again that same helpless inability to control myself. We experience unpredictable reactions all the time, less dramatically. A casual remark hurts our feelings: we become angry, we do not know why. The reasons lie beyond our conscious recall; our un-Christlike responses are triggered by buried memories in the subconscious. This then is exactly why we need to be reborn. Our return to the God-image has to extend beyond conscious assent to those areas of our being which are the wellspring of our conduct, the source of our motives and drives.

The new birth, without doubt, takes place at a precise moment, as does conception, but the moment may be equally unrecorded. The new quality of life that possesses the spiritually-made-alive takes over the personality at varying rates. I once read of a notorious harlot who, stopping to listen to a street evangelist, was changed almost instantaneously to a woman of virtue. A man in our town was so evidently reborn that his Jewish neighbor remarked, "It was like a resurrection." On the other hand, we have seen the less spectacular, though clearly perceptible, growth of other Christians.

It is not enough, therefore, to possess personality—every human person does—but we must surrender our entire being to God, to be changed from glory to glory until we grow into the image of Christ. Therefore, our first obligation as stewards of personality, I believe, is to accept the new birth, each according to the pattern of our lives. This is our commitment to God's need for "wondrous being."

We *are* stewardesses. We have no option. We can only choose the fashion in which we practice our stewardship. We recognize, of course, that our control of circumstances and surroundings is limited. Since the bounds of potential personality are set by heredity, education, health, and the times in which we live, self-control and self-determination have their limits. By surrendering ourselves and our circumstances to God we actually increase the extent to which we control our lives. Jesus demonstrated the completely God-controlled personality.

Our development as persons does depend in a measure upon definite things we can will:

We can will to believe. This is the foundation stone of all our relations to God.

We can will to receive "the manifold grace of God," for the Lord gives only to those who open their hearts to Him.

We can will to live expectantly, for God delights in working for the good of those who love Him.

We can will to open our consciousness to God, that we may experience His presence.

We can will to open our consciousness to other persons, that we may receive from them and give to them.

Stewardship is more than holding in trust. It is the willingness to receive, that we may have to share. It is assuming responsibility to become better stewardesses of whatever God has entrusted to us. It is even daring to ask for larger opportunity in the kingdom without craving personal success on the one hand, or being haunted by fear of failure on the other.

Discovering who we really are is a necessary part of being able to use well what God has given us. You may recall Oliver Wendell Holmes' illustration of the six persons always present when two persons enter into dialogue:

X as X thinks he is.	Y as Y thinks he is.
X as Y thinks he is.	Y as X thinks he is.
X as God knows X is.	Y as God knows Y is.

To discover that person God knows us to be is further complicated by the images reflected back to us from countless persons about us. Visualize this by imagining you are making a drawing.

1. Draw a reasonable silhouette of yourself, something like the figures on a measurements chart, letting your body represent you as God would have you be.

2. Superimpose on this, as shaded figures, the images others have of you—the people who matter, as parents, husband, your children, your employer, your pastor. To your child you may be mostly bosom and hands, to your pupils mostly head. These will be distorted figures.

3. Draw outline figures showing how you think about yourself in relation to these same persons, again with honest distortions, for we do like certain people to believe we are what we know we are not.

The more nearly all these shadow images conform to God's model figure, the more satisfactory we find life. We sometimes cling to our false selves because it is painful to grow into God's image. The more nearly these false figures become conformed to the God-envisioned one, the stronger will be our power to help those around us, for unity within produces unity without. Honesty and sincerity before God and man are essential in growth of personality. By thoughtful aloneness, by abandonment to prayer, by ruthless exposure of our deepest desires to His scrutiny (to remove our fears of their validity or to reveal to us their shoddiness) we can find our true selves, the personalities God had in mind when He willed us to be.

Listen with your mind's ear. You can hear a troupe of children wailing, "Let me *be*," in response to teasing, or worse. Perhaps you can hear the refrain in your own consciousness, expressed in one way or another, as pressure of various kinds have bruised and battered you. "Let me *be*" is an idiom growing out of human experience. Wanting to *be*, to be ourselves, to *become* is as natural in a healthy personality as wanting to grow taller and more mature. We may not all have had growing pains in the body, but we all know the inevitable pains of growing mentally, socially, and spiritually. It takes character to bear this suffering, or see it borne, without running for an aspirin or a tranquilizer or retreating to invalidism.

Sometimes this wail becomes an ungrammatical "Leave me *alone*," especially among the young. Unknowingly, they are demanding the right of individuality, the right from the pressures that bind and distort. Of course we know each generation has to pass on the disciplines that shape the next, even if they prove, in our rapidly changing culture, to be shortsighted fully as often as farsighted. Two things we need to remember: we may need to fight for the privacy our souls must have for growing; we must help provide for others the privacy they need.

I once read of a woman who lived in close quarters with many children. She had no place of retreat, no closet with a door. So, wise woman, she trained her children that when "Mother has her apron over her head" she must not be disturbed. So precious is aloneness, so urgent is its necessity in being and becoming persons.

This matter of finding and accepting our own peculiar gifts and handicaps is Scriptural. (Read Romans 12:1-8 in several versions.) It is also a matter of spiritual discernment. It has to be, for there is a very fine line between (borrowing Phillips' phrasing) not cherishing "exaggerated ideas of yourself," and having a "sane estimate of your capabilities."

Because personality is so complex we are often confused by our own actions and attitudes. We find it difficult to distinguish within ourselves self-pity and self-justification on the one hand and sensible evaluation of our limitations on the other; between undue elation and just satisfaction; between presumption and daring faith; between caution and cowardice; between righteousness and Pharisaism. And so on and on.

We need the "light of faith" for this transformation and renewing of the mind, Romans recommends. It is no less sinful to carry a dwarfed, anemic image of oneself (used to excuse us from work God intends us to do) than an unhealthily bloated one (used to intrude ourselves into work God never intended us to do). Perhaps part of the secret of being a healthy organ in the body of Christ is to accept sane estimates from our friends and be willing to give sane estimates in return. When we solicit praise or listen only to flattery, we err. When we reject sincere compliments and cherish slurs, we err.

Fear of hurt pride (because we *can't* shine) can keep us from cultivating our less obvious facets of personality. Fear of hurt pride (because we *won't* shine) can keep us from sharing our already discovered ones.

Admittedly, the man who invested ten talents was in danger of becoming materialistic and spoiled by success, but he took the risk and received the highest praise. The man who wrapped his talent in a napkin, thinking to secure himself from failure, received unqualified blame. The only solution is to bring ourselves again and again honestly to the Lord, to have Him separate between meekness and mousiness, between confidence and complacency.

There is a fine line, too, between doing a thing to express our personalities and doing it for the honor of the Lord. The line is so fine that we may even end up specializing in lowly service so that we will be praised for lowly service. Or a teacher, "so wonderful with children," may teach with joy disciplined children in a well-equipped nursery but disdain grimy urchins in a backwoods chapel or storefront church, because she is more interested in running her little circus than in forming character in children. If we can do fine embroidery that calls forth satisfying praise, we must remember that the Lord may also send us overalls to patch, perhaps without the satisfaction of praise.

Your unique gift may be your cross. It may lead you to the place where your singleness of purpose to honor the Lord crosses the prevailing pattern of your segment of society. The same originality that your friends praise in your kitchen curtains or your casseroles may also require you to express the "originality of the Spirit." Your friends do not have to copy your curtains or your casseroles, so you do not threaten them there; but your current insight on the role of the Christian in PTA may be costly to you and to them because it requires action.

Strangely, you will perhaps find it harder to develop your

own pattern of spirituality than any other facet of your personality. There are always pressures to push us one way or another. But Jesus said, "I am the way." So if we are possessed by His Spirit, as we should be, His way working itself out through our personalities and circumstances is bound to be different from that of every other person so possessed and so living. If you do not believe this, being paralyzed by a loyalty to what you have taught to be "the way," write down quickly the names of ten persons undebatably recognized as "Christian" despite their differences in theology or life philosophy. Or list the authors of your ten favorite hymns. Study your lists, noting the variety of spiritual expression you will certainly find in these persons of the way.

Perhaps these to whom the presence of God must be real to be satisfying suffer most in our activistic times. We are urged on every hand to *go,* to *do,* to *tell.* We are told that "a mystical sort of being, without going" is less than Christian. Could it not also be that going without being, going without the sense of His presence, going without a knowledge that the spiritual is the real, is also less than Christian? If your soul thrives on quiet and meditation, if you honestly accept a ministry of intercession as service, why force yourself to express your devotion in a round of activity? The important thing is to discover and follow your spiritual bent, seeking to share in ways compatible to your personality.

The exciting thing about God using personality is that each of us is capable of experiencing truth in a way that no other individual has. That is more than exciting; it is overwhelming because of the responsibility it carries. It is particularly meaningful for women, because traditionally they have been the silent ones, asking their husbands at home.

At the moment, I can think of one woman whose voice is respectfully listened to in the financial world and one such woman in theological circles. Not many women attain stature in politics. Women who star in literature, art, music, and administration are proportionately few. Think through the Bible stories, however, and you will see that there have always been women whose character and excellence set them apart.

Some time ago a minister, while eloquently describing how it would be if mankind would fully respond to God's longing to reveal Himself, said, "Every woman bowed over the washtub would have her ear cocked to the Word of God here and now." We may ask, "What is she to do with the Word she receives?" Many will answer, "Receive it. Live it. Pass it on by example to those she influences."

The instinctive answer seems peculiarly suited to feminine personality. Comfortably, it saves women-at-large from guilt for not "speaking out," for not "grabbing a soapbox." Yet we can agree with the wisdom of an African proverb that says, "Women are the keepers of the community." So women historians will continue to tell the stories that knit the generations. Women poets will continue to point out sunsets and cultivate a sensitivity in relationships. Women musicians will croon lullabys and slip on the better records lest only trivial tastes develop. Women artists will continue to arrange flowers and furniture, devise becoming clothes, and create new dishes. Churchwomen will continue to teach Sunday school and cook the fellowship suppers. None of this will be earth-shaking or sky-probing, but how poor the world would be if all this good were mass-produced by a committee or a bureau, instead of being practiced in every cottage and ranch house, in every chapel and church.

But let us not forget: there are some women to whom God has given the more public station. Let us beware, lest we undercut God's purpose for them. Such women more often attain their roles by recognized excellence than by engineered election. Many of them have had the character to grasp the opportunities thrust upon them by rigorous circumstances while their weaker sisters retreated into comfortable convention and convenience. What God has given such women is a trust, to them and to us, for we must uphold them in their stewardship.

SHARING ONE'S PERSONALITY

We can control, within limits, how much of our personality we want to share, how much of ourselves we want to give away. Imagine yourself alone in a railroad station hundreds of miles from home. A strange man sitting nearby in some way, by appearance or action, arouses your suspicions. By your very posture and the tones of your voice when you answer him in monosyllables, you build and maintain a wall between you. Then you look up to see the man-next-door approaching, for he also has been on a journey. What a different reception you give him! Similarly, within a group you can elect to give of yourself or to withdraw into your preoccupations, or reservations, or imagined inferiorities. You can accept stewardship of any encounter or reject it.

The Lomas of Liberia have an idea that when you have expressed a bad thought it runs around independently, stirring up trouble. They have a point! Even unexpressed hostile thoughts can act like a virus in a group. Unseen, they infect every personality open to infection. Enthusiasm and good will, expressed or even unexpressed, are also catching. The "atmosphere of the meeting" we talk about is created by whatever the personalities there give of themselves. Adding to this composite effect is how we "contribute by just being there," as we are often urged to do. Belief and approval and concern are infectious. This is why we have members' meetings and small prayer groups when we want close, warm sharing. Unbelief and hostility and apathy are infectious. This is why some groups ask any person not in accord with their purposes to leave a special prayer meeting. Obviously, it is only good stewardship of personality to take our share of the responsibility for the success of any group occasion.

Christians are finding that they can will to liberate the love within them for the healing of others. A certain lady, admirable in many ways, had peculiarities which made her hard to love. When adversities piled themselves upon her, her reactions to her troubles further alienated her from her neighbors. Although people pitied her, they found it hard to experience Christian compassion and genuine concern. One woman said, "We must *consciously* love her," and so some women gathered and willed to send out love to her as they prayed. The woman's attitude to her problem changed. Her neighbors' attitude toward her changed. The problem itself was solved far beyond

87

the expectations of all. "Learn how to utilize the fiber and core of your heart," advised Dr. Dooley. This gift lies peculiarly in the province of women.

Being bombarded, as we are, with statistics telling us how many thousands have been added to the population since we got up this morning, we find it hard to take our individual worth in the world seriously. The best remedy I have found for the sensation of disappearing into nothingness when I hear that soon I will be 1/3,000,000,000 of the world's population is to think of the power packed into the atom. If I release my atom's power of good within the circle of my influence, and if all the other persons of good will in the world will do the same, these circles of love will merge eventually. The world will actually have a better atmosphere because we have released "the love . . . shed abroad in our hearts." As other persons associate with us personally, or are reached by letter or even hearsay, they receive of our values, our motives, our graces. When we will to share of ourselves, this influence is enlarged in extent and deepened in intensity.

FEMININE FACETS OF PERSONALITY

A part of the evaluation we must make of our personality is an inventory of what makes us stewardesses instead of stewards. What have we to give an account of that men do not share? It is time that we women each make an effort to recognize and use, and thus demonstrate and validate, the gifts for which women excel. In what ways can a woman be man's helpmate besides rocking his baby and sewing on his buttons, or keeping his files in order, or serving as a model for his version of "Whistler's Mother"?

Some time ago I read an article—written with tongue-in-cheek, I suspect—arguing that women will have to take to government if the world is not eventually to be blown to bits. It told of two men overheard discussing whether this would happen if an atomic bomb were exploded under certain conditions. "We'll never know until we try it," one said. So, concluded the author, woman's compassion for people, her concern for the welfare of all, must come to the rescue of man, who is being carried away by scientific interest, love of power, jealousy of prestige.

We admire the mechanical, analytical, financial, administrative gifts of men, which admittedly exceed our own. But these need to be balanced by compassionate concern, regard for relationships, sensitivity to beauty, and that elusive factor that combines into "the woman's touch." Women have always managed by indirection to contribute these qualities. In this age we have a peculiar opportunity and obligation to deliberately use our gifts. Not being so involved in protecting imaginary boundaries of dignity, we can think of lives lost, bodies maimed, personalities stunted and twisted by the hates of war and strife. Not easily related to programs and projects, we can detect the chill of cold philanthropy. In this day when organization can easily become a fetish, woman's quick compassion is needed to keep the wheels of social and ecclesiastical machinery from obscuring the cause of those for whom the wheels were set in motion, lest persons be sacrificed to policies and politics.

A woman's character as a woman can perhaps be measured by the quality of her maternal concern. A half-wit mother instinctively shows fierce concern for her child by protecting him from physical danger, and by keeping him near her, even when not for his future good. There are, on the other hand, intelligent, devoted mothers who sacrifice the physical presence of their children (and sometimes of their husbands) for long periods of time that the work of the kingdom may go on.

We know, too, of women, like Mary Slessor or the Small Woman, who have put away the thought and opportunity of marriage to serve alone in isolated corners of the world. It takes special grace to extend vicariously our maternal love to faceless, formless beings of whom we have merely heard. It also takes special dedication to minister to the unlovely person next door. We have not truly dedicated our capacity for motherliness until it is expendable for any and all, whether repulsively near or nebulously far.

Take also this matter of what is indulgently or otherwise referred to as woman's intuition. Since a girl's acceptance as a

89

valued member of the family, both in her father's house and in her married home, has depended on her ability to please, it is natural that she cultivate an eye for the change of color, the tensing of muscles, the slight gestures that communicate without words. It has been to her advantage to sense currents of feeling that flow between members of her household. A girl-child probably has no wide edge on a boy-child in this respect, but our society has encouraged a boy to put "facts" before feeling and "demonstrate evidence" before observation. Hence he grows up to quote investigators and draw sociograms, while she "knows" (if she is a mother) that Johnnie is developing into a lone wolf, or (if she is a secretary) that Mr. Boss despises Mr. Colleague, in spite of his careful display of back-slapping.

A churchman, who has more than usual insight in this realm, once said that if an emergency requires a snap decision, it is well to trust the woman's. For centuries women have been pulling children out of the fire and away from the fire (literally and figuratively), while the men have made long-range plans to confine the fire or have sought to discover the psychological attraction of fire for children, so that they can remove the inner causes. Both approaches are useful in society.

This ability to sum up a situation and apply a quick solution does not commend itself, of course, to all the problems of the day; but perhaps intuition and compassion can point the direction of search for desirable change. The child needs to be got from the fire while his burns are still first-degree, curable by home remedies, and even a silly method is better than leaving him there until he has to be hospitalized at public expense. A homemade extinguisher has some advantages over an elaborate system yet to be installed.

RESPONSIBILITY FOR THE PERSONALITY OF OTHERS

A part of our stewardship of personality, as hinted before, is the cherishing and nourishing of the personality of others. Help we can give to start another on a satisfying career that "just fits his personality" is one of the most precious gifts we can give. Women have this opportunity often, as they deal with their own children or work with children in other capacities. Highly to be praised is the sweetheart or the wife, mother or sister, who encourages a man to take the dangerous hard way to the career to which he feels drawn, rather than to take a short cut to a quick-paying job or to stay in an economically safe position he already has. Most highly to be praised is she who undergirds a man's decision to leave the usual conventional patterns of church service for more daring heights of spiritual leadership—sometimes unsung, often misunderstood and criticized. Not less fruitful can be the same sort of service rendered to another woman or girl.

THAT SPECIAL FACET

Reams of papers, yea, shelves of books, have been written to extol the power of women to stir the pulses and purposes of men. It all sounds fairy and airy and romantic and inspirational. But the hard light of everyday experience and observation reveals that this ultimate of gifts carries the ultimate of dangers. The face that can launch a fleet or precipitate a war can also destroy homes and ruin lives. It therefore requires some special consecration in the heart. A mature Christian woman who read a much-discussed book based on the sex tangles of a community to see what it had to say to Christians, commented that if she would go around her predominantly "Christian" town, revealing everything of the sort there, she could write such a book, too. Surely we need to consider the stewardship of sex appeal.

We know that a man's ego is flattered by his power to attract women. A woman's ego is flattered by her power to attract men. So it seems to me the secret to good stewardship of sex appeal is to see to it that this element of the ego, along with what certain peoples term "body-hunger," is presented as a living sacrifice to Christ. It is relatively easy to sing, "Jesus satisfies my every longing," but it is something else again to surrender these deep, deep, demanding hungers to spiritual fulfillment—for that means surrendering the demands of the ego, to deny biological prerogatives. It seems that to do so is to give up the wholeness of one's self. But on

91

the contrary when she has done it, the woman finds herself to be not a female first of all, but a person first of all. Thus her surrender does not de-sex her, but frees her from the tyranny of sex, making her more whole (and wholesome) because she can unself-consciously give of her distinctly feminine gifts to the enrichment of the body of Christ. She can, like the "sisters" Paul commends, contribute as "neither male nor female." She can, for instance, pray fervently for the needs of a Christian man without a nagging question of whether her motives are pure. She can then be a wall and a tower—a source of strength —and not a door—an entrance into temptation. This path is a hard fine line that requires much soul-searching and surrender with faith that Christ can fulfill natural desires by transposing them into their spiritual counterparts.

We sometimes thought (before the day of confessions magazines) the married woman less vulnerable to the attractions of other men because she had found her fulfillment in her husband. Similarly, the woman fully surrendered to and possessed by the love of God should find within herself no inner demand to use womanly wiles for her own flattery.

Does not the ultimate in womanly satisfaction come from the ultimate in surrender, in being utterly possessed? Are these not also the ultimates in spiritual relationship with God? Let the natural become the parable and the figure of the spiritual. Do not suppress imagination as evil, but ask the Lord to transpose the imagined fulfillment of the natural into the real fulfillment of the spiritual. No one but God can know, but perhaps they who are deprived of the natural may in the end more truly comprehend the spiritual union of which the saints have written. Certainly not all the willingly celibate from Saint Paul down to our day were deluded.

We should protect ourselves from the sins of sex by the armor of Christ's spirit within, not by clamping on a chastity belt of grim determination lest we incur the wrath of God and disgrace ourselves in society. Christ, our Elder Brother, was seen with harlots and allowed grateful women to bathe His feet and pour perfume on His head. If He was not subject to temptation, He was an impostor and the Scriptures untruthful.

His armor was complete submission to God. He had no "lust to entice" from within, and so temptation had no grip upon Him from without.

When woman surrenders to God her peculiar powers and instincts and finds them purified, she is free to use them fully for the kingdom—or even completely for her husband and family. If a woman is burdened with a sense of second-rate-ness, "of blame and shame," that faulty training and mores have forced upon her, or fears the unleashed strength of the deep powers within herself, she cannot be her whole self or give her whole self.

Along with the several usual interpretations given to Jesus' rebuke to Martha and His defense of Mary, there is another that appeals to me. Martha chose to honor and support Him by the usual giving of food and comfort—first thought of women. Apparently, she wanted to do it well, maybe with sub-conscious satisfaction in her gifts as a hostess. Mary, sitting at Jesus' feet, gave Him the support of a sympathetic audience. I can imagine that Jesus' own thoughts came clearer, as He watched Mary's face for her comprehension of the ageless truths He spoke and her sensing of the fateful possibilities these truths had for Him. Mary's gift was a part of her very personality.

> Two women met Him at the door.
> One gave Him bread.
> (He could have bought it at the inn,
>   or begged it from the village slut.)
> The other gave courageous love,
>   a listening ear.
> He went away, His spirit strong.
> (And He was God!)

Mary's "part" seems to me to be the pinnacle of a woman's self-giving when performed "as unto Christ" "unto the least of these."

A woman's voluntary resolution to give this ultimate, inti-mate part of feminine personality to the enrichment of the kingdom, to the endowment of the body of Christ (whichever figure is the most stimulating), takes the mockery out of the oft-repeated admonition to the single and childless to "sublimate" her instincts to mate and bear children. (For to this admonition is appended the note that one cannot sublimate for the sake of sublimation; self-sacrificing, hence self-satisfying substitution must spring from deeper motives.) She is assured that her natural inclinations to nurture, to comfort, to inspire, when thus consecrated to the good of all mankind, become useful in the spiritual kingdom as surely as if they were exerted in the natural sense. While she knows this same privilege can be realized by her married sisters, her joy is that she has not been denied the "better part," the eternal reasons for her being, that in fact the Scripture that "the barren shall have more children than she who is married" is not just Eastern poetry.

To a Protestant, the vows of a Catholic nun seem hard, unnatural, unnecessary. But her way may be the easier (at the first look), for having cut off the possibility of marriage, she at least can lay aside the tentativeness which plagues many girls most of their lives. Yet, unless she, too, truly finds how to transpose her natural desires into spiritual ones, she has the same problem. In the meanwhile the Protestant woman has the more stringent role, for she must practice her denial of feminine ego in the midst of society, regardless of possible reversal of circumstances. If single, or if married, she is God's, eschewing the negative restrictions and taboos, foregoing tawdry triumphs for the higher motivation of being a good stewardess of her "help-meetness."

PERSONALITY FOR GOD'S HONOR

The church has not yet taken seriously, I think, the resources of feminine personality. Someone has pointed out that the same passage which exhorts women to simplicity, also urges men to "lift holy hands in prayer." In a well-balanced human body both masculine and feminine sex characteristics interplay, yet it cannot function normally unless one or the other predominates. In a well-balanced personality the attributes commonly ascribed both to men and to women are found, but to be acceptable to society and conducive of happiness to the individual, one set must predominate. Is it not therefore reasonable to believe that the body of Christ—the church—will be most efficient when feminine gifts are recognized as equally essential to masculine ones, though instinct, common sense, and almost universal custom agree on which shall be dominant. There is no quarrel concerning leadership if it be worthy of "followship"!

Women will continue to use their special gifts, whether asked for or not, whether taken for granted or sought out. But in this age of "equality" (the merits of which of course are debatable), when women are given more and more recognition in secular fields, we need the undergirding of honest recognition by the church to give us a sense of validity commensurate to the responsibilities entrusted to us.

Sometimes the Lord calls a woman to unusual service in the church. This has caused much question in the hearts of some who accept Paul's warnings and overlook his endorsements of "sisters" and "mothers in Israel" and his recognition of Priscilla's role in his life; who overlook also Philip's four daughters, who were recognized messengers of the Lord, and Lydia, who laid the foundation of a church by leading a prayer group. But fiercest of all can be the conflict in the heart of the especially called one herself. One such was Mrs. Penn-Lewis, an Englishwoman who over the turn of the century entered many doors of service, public as well as private, in England, Finland, and Russia. Out of much prayer and seeking with God's seal on her work, she wrote:

"In the home sphere she is woman, wife, mother, sister; but in the church and in the service of God, praying or 'proclaiming godliness,' she is a 'partaker of the divine nature,' a messenger of the Lord of hosts, a member of the heavenly body of the church—in both spheres seeking, with a meek and quiet spirit, to do the will of her head in heaven."

That Mrs. Penn-Lewis fulfilled her ideal is shown by the incident in which a "gentleman with strong prejudice against the ministry of women" came to her after a meeting to say:

"I would not have believed it possible, had I not seen it, that God would use a *woman* like that!"

Her answer underscores the basis of such an unusual ministry: "God never does use a woman like that, *or a man either!* God only uses the *new creation.*"

PERSONALITY—FROM GOD TO GOD

So as true stewardesses, we take up the challenge of giving ourselves to God, not only as we now are, but as He envisions us capable of becoming. As God invades our personalities—at our invitation—His presence within changes us, renewing our minds, purifying our affections, raising our goals, giving us grace to surrender consciously to His control the unconscious depths beyond our control. As we grow "from grace to grace," we will, like Jesus, inevitably come into conflict with evil—perhaps in high places, if not in the low. Inevitably we will choose to let die some of our most treasured facets of personality and rights as an individual. But from this willingly buried self, God will bring new life—within ourselves, within the body of Christ, within the world—whether we realize it now or must wait to see it hereafter. This is the road of faith for the stewardess.

About the Writer

Elizabeth A. Showalter, the daughter of a minister and the youngest in a family of 12, was born near Broadway, Virginia, where she grew up. As big brothers married, the business of being an aunt became a large part of Elizabeth's life. She graduated from Eastern Mennonite College, received her B.S. from Madison College, taught in the public schools of Virginia and later at Iowa Mennonite High School. In 1949 she arrived at the Mennonite Publishing House as editor of *Words of Cheer* and became "Aunt Beth" to hundreds of her readers. While here she also wrote curriculum materials. Of her recent experience teaching crafts to women and children at Penn Alps she said, "I love it. I want to teach the rest of my fifties, write

96

books like Laura Ingalls Wilder in my sixties, paint like Grandma Moses in my seventies, and weave in my eighties. Actually, of course, I know the Lord has His own schedule, which I shall have to discover step by step." The next step proved to be the Syracuse University School of Journalism.

STEWARDSHIP *of intellect is a joy.*
Let us commit our minds to it
for the glory of God.
                              —Elaine Rich.

6

STEWARDSHIP OF INTELLECT

ELAINE SOMMERS RICH

ONE of God's significant gifts to us is intellect, intelligence, mind. Every human being, including the retardate, possesses this gift, although the quality varies greatly from person to person. We are not responsible to God for the amount of intelligence with which we are natively endowed. But we are responsible to God for the use we make of whatever intelligence we have.

Intelligence is difficult to define. Guilford has suggested that there are about fifty known factors of the intellect. Others may be yet unknown. Getzels and Jackson prefer to separate it into modes. The first has to do with retaining the known, learning the predetermined, and conserving what is. The second has to do with revising the known, exploring the undetermined, and constructing what might be. They call the first *intelligence* and the second *creativity*.[1] This essay will include both these facets of mind in the term *intellect*.

Even as we attempt to discuss stewardship of intellect, we must be aware that we are trying to isolate what can only be isolated in the world of words, not in the world of not-words. The ancient Greek philosophers divided man into parts. Aristotle called these *ethos, logos,* and *pathos* (character, mind, emotion). But the Hebrew conception was different and probably nearer the truth.

In the Old Testament passages where the English word "mind" appears and the idea of thinking occupies an impor-

99

tant place, it is primarily thinking related to action, either recalled from the past or planned for the future.[2] Jesus also thought of personality as a unity. "The light of the body is the eye: if therefore thine eye be single, thy whole body shall be full of light" (Matthew 6:22).

Although we here attempt to separate "intellect" long enough to discuss it, we must realize that in everyday living stewardship of intellect frequently requires moving the muscles of the hands, legs, or tongue!

Where then shall we exercise stewardship of intelligence? We shall mention four areas.

AT HOME

Let us begin at home with our households. Stewardship of intellect requires that we periodically analyze what we are doing and place it under the judgment of Christ. Tentmaking is secondary; extending the kingdom is primary. If Christian women can by using their minds decrease the time that goes into "tentmaking," at the same time preserving the quality of the tent, then they should do so.

For example, teaching the Christian faith to children, visiting the sick and elderly, and working for legislation favorable toward world peace are all activities more important than dusting furniture. Yet clean homes are necessary to good living. If the Christian woman can cut her dusting time a third by using two dustcloths at the same time, one in each hand, then she should do so. If she is preparing a grocery shopping list, she may as well list items in the order in which they are arranged in the store. This stewardship of intellect may cut her shopping time in half. Planning menus a week at a time, rather than a day or meal at a time, results in similar saving. By concentrating rather than scattering mental effort, the household manager achieves greater inner freedom. She seems to create for herself more time and psychic energy to devote to the kingdom, for discipline is the gateway to freedom.

As an outstanding example in this area we may cite Dr. Lillian M. Gilbreth, mother of the famous dozen. She pioneered in applying management principles and techniques at home. *Living with Our Children* (Norton), first published in 1928, remains contemporary reading.

Another area in which we should solve problems, see relationships, visualize with our minds what should be, is congregational life. Does a congregation exist anywhere which could not become a better witness to Christ by improved stewardship of intellect?

We are not lone Christians thinking, independent of others. We are members of one another. We possess gifts not for ourselves alone, but for the upbuilding of the entire congregation. If we refuse to exercise our gifts on behalf of the congregation, we sin. For example, if a woman sees a glaring blind spot in the Christian education program of her congregation and what could be done about it, yet refuses to speak, she is not exercising good stewardship of intellect. For the sake of the church, she should speak, humbly, for she may be wrong. A prophet is not responsible to God for those who refuse to hear him, but he is responsible if he refuses to speak.

The following passages of Scripture deal with group stewardship of mind:

KJV

Be of the same mind one toward another. Romans 12:16a

That ye may with one mind and one mouth glorify God, even the Father of our Lord Jesus Christ. Romans 15:6

Now I beseech you, brethren, by the name of our Lord Jesus Christ, that ye all speak the same

RSV

Live in harmony with one another.

. . . that together you may with one voice glorify the God and Father of our Lord Jesus Christ.

I appeal to you, brethren, by the name of our Lord Jesus Christ, that all of you agree and that

101

thing, and that there be no divisions among you; but that ye be perfectly joined together in the same mind and in the same judgment. I Corinthians 1:10

there be no dissensions among you, but that you be united in the same mind and the same judgment.

The kind of agreement Paul speaks of in these passages is impossible without face-to-face encounter and discussion. For this reason it is well to review here the steps in group problem-solving.

Step One: Define and analyze the problem.

Questions of fact cannot be solved by group discussion. They can be solved only by research to determine fact. Questions of policy do lend themselves to group solution.

1. Examples of questions of fact: How many children were enrolled in our summer Bible school last year? What percentage of the economy in our state is oriented to military "needs"?

2. Examples of questions of policy: How can we improve our summer Bible school during the coming year? How can the military-oriented portion of the economy in our state convert to peace-oriented economy?

Step Two: List all possible solutions to the problem.

At this point we are often lazy. We list only two either-or solutions. Red or dead. Traditional or modern. Relief or missions. Defense contracts or unemployment. Fortunately for His children, in God there are infinite possibilities, infinite combinations, infinite variety. Through group stewardship of intellect we open our minds to the guidance of the Holy Spirit. Congregations are often amazed to discover a solution they had not dreamed of when they went into a particular problem.

Step Three: Test the solutions with facts.

If a congregation is working, for example, on resettling a refugee family into its midst, it will need information, facts, about the following: What are the job possibilities? What are the housing possibilities? What can we provide in the way of language tutoring?

Evidence from history may help. How have we done this in the past? Opinions of the "experts," those who have more information and experience in this particular problem, may be valuable.

Step Four: Select the best solution.

At this step, knowledge of what has happened before may not be enough. Here we especially need the ability to create first with our minds what will later become reality.

Step Five: Put it into action.

This requires faith and work.

A Christian congregation should be a model of stewardship of intellect.

IN THE ARTS

The arts are a third area in which Christians are stewards of intellect. We are all consumers of the arts. We sing. We listen. We hang pictures on our walls. We read. We place upon our shelves objects to contemplate or enjoy. What kind of art does our consumption encourage?

Ernest Gordon in his moving testimony to the power of God, *Through the Valley of the Kwai* (Harper, 1962), tells of how spiritual renewal in the prison camps of southeast Asia was paralleled by a remarkable upsurge of creativity in the arts.

Creativity in the arts is a response to the grace of God. We must somehow express what we feel. We must share with other people what we have come to understand about life. We long to "sing unto the Lord a new song."

The artist awakens us to aspects of reality we might otherwise miss. The artist deepens our awareness. The artist helps us to live more abundantly. Let us then release the artist in ourselves. Let us encourage and cherish our artists.

IN COMMUNITY LIFE

A fourth area in which stewardship of intellect manifests itself is community life at various levels, local to international.

103

One expects that where there is Christian stewardship of intellect, there will also be libraries, good schools, adequate recreational and medical facilities, a just economic system, and, above all, peaceful relations among nations.

HOW IT IS EXERCISED

In order to exercise stewardship of intellect, it is necessary to place into the schedule time for individual and group study. This is done in various ways.

The Mormons (Church of Jesus Christ of the Latter-day Saints) are fond of the sentence, "Intelligence is the glory of God." Local units of their Women's Relief Society meet once a week, usually on a weekday morning. Their study program follows a four-area cycle. One meeting per month is devoted to the study of theology; a second deals with practical problems, such as bread baking or home nursing; a third is devoted to the study of literature, e.g., "The Challenge of Walt Whitman"; and a fourth meeting per month is given to a social science study. This is an adult education program carried on by the church. It is impossible to calculate the value of such a study program over a period of years to the individual and the group.

Those Christians who follow the Kirkridge Discipline (Headquarters at Bangor, Pennsylvania) agree as part of their discipline to the following:

"Study. Reading for intellectual growth and a sounder understanding of the faith that is within us the equivalent of at least a solid book monthly, to interpret past and present in Christian maturity."

Yokefellows (Headquarters at 223 College Avenue, Richmond, Indiana) also include study in their discipline. They consider as a part of Christ's yoke "Study—development in intellectual integrity by careful study of Christian books."

The Jewish people say, "The law stands on three legs—worship, study, and good deeds." In the Talmud is a saying interpreted by Rabbi Jonah as follows: "Where there is no one wiser than you, 'strive to be a man,' that is, do not give up trying to increase in wisdom; even though you do not find in your city someone wiser than you, consider: what if you were a contemporary of the Talmudic Sages and were in their company! . . . Thus you will never neglect to study, and every single day you will improve your conduct, for you will be increasing in wisdom and will be like an ever-flowing stream."[3] Study is a part of the Jewish religion.

Wherever the good news of Christ has gone, literacy, books, and libraries have also gone. Stewardship of intellect means study. Study means schools, books, and libraries.

It should be noted that a Christian community is strengthened when its members share the fruits of their study with one another. Christians need one another in the task of vanquishing the wilderness of ignorance in which we live.

At the local level the Sunday-school class should be such a place of sharing. Here we should be students of the Bible and creative visualizers of how the message of God can be applied in our day. Suppose adults were given grades for their work in Sunday-school classes as their children and grandchildren are given grades in school. Would A's, C's, or F's predominate? Where there is Christian stewardship of intellect, such aids to Bible study as commentaries and dictionaries not only become available; they are also eventually produced.

The mode of intellect described earlier as "revising the known, exploring the undetermined, and constructing what might be" also requires time and apparent leisure. It is necessary that we place into our schedules time for creative thought and activity and that we respect such time in other people's schedules. A novelist explained that she wrote most of her book on the golf course because her friends respected her right to be uninterrupted while playing golf!

OBSTACLES

What are the obstacles to Christian stewardship of intellect? They are outer and inner.

The major outer enemy is a social climate of anti-intellectualism in which activities such as knitting or bowling may be considered more acceptable than studying either a foreign language or the economics of disarmament. In such an atmosphere it may be more acceptable to collect salt and pepper shakers than to buy original art works. The only way to conquer this enemy is to have the God-given courage to oppose such social pressure.

The inner and greater enemy is laziness. During medieval times it was called sloth and counted one of the seven deadly sins. *Lazy* suggests a disinclination or aversion to work. *Indolent* describes a habitual love of ease and a settled dislike of movement or activity.

How hard it is for us to change! How we love our comfortable ruts! How we shrink from the risk that goes with being creative! We had rather bury our one talent of intelligence at home. Then there will be no mistakes, no getting into trouble with the authorities, no criticism from others. We feel that we are somehow special, different from other people. They can do things; we cannot. We shrink from calling this attitude what it is, sin. And sin takes its toll. The spiritual principle is true. If we refuse to be good stewards, even that which we have is taken away from us.

REWARDS

What then are the rewards, the fruits, of good stewardship of intellect? They are the upbuilding of the Christian community, the kingdom of God at work as it should be in the world, and joy for the individual.

For a Christian woman marriage is neither requisite nor hindrance to stewardship of intellect. We reject the idea that if a woman wishes to use her mind she must renounce husband, home, and children. If she has been called into marriage, then stewardship of intellect is not only a service in itself but also a kind of insurance. It guarantees that when her children reach maturity and launch out on their own, she will be equipped to continue a fruitful period of service to God and the Christian community.

Stewardship of intellect is in no sense a grim obligation. It is a joy. Christ's yoke is easy and His burden is light. Let us then commit our minds to Him to use for His glory.

106

About the Writer

Elaine Sommers Rich (Mrs. Ronald) grew up in Plevna, Indiana. She received a B.A. from Goshen College, an M.A. from Michigan State University. Before marrying Ronald Rich, who teaches chemistry at Bethel College, North Newton, Kansas, she taught English at Goshen College. They are the parents of Jonathan (10), Andrew (9), Miriam (6), and Mark (2½). Elaine edited the book, *Breaking Bread Together*, and wrote a novel for young people, *Hannah Elizabeth*. She has also been housemother for eight years in a small college dormitory.

FOOTNOTES

1. Jacob W. Getzels and Philip W. Jackson, *Creativity and Intelligence* (John Wiley and Sons, 1962), p. 13 f.
2. R. C. Denton in the *Interpreter's Dictionary of the Bible* (Abingdon, 1962), Vol. 3, p. 383.
3. *The Living Talmud* (Mentor, 1957), p. 92 f.

GOD *is glorified by the speech of the Christian in that He takes weak and fallible human beings, and so infills them with His redeeming love and so blesses their testimony by the work of His Spirit in the hearts of the hearers that men are drawn to God.*

—J. C. Wenger, in *Separated unto God.*

STEWARDSHIP OF SPEECH

MARY REMPEL

SIZE does not always determine importance.

"Think of ships," writes James, "large they may be, yet even when driven by strong gales they can be directed by a tiny rudder" (3:4, NEB). Tiny it is indeed, when compared in size and weight to the great vessel it commands.

"So with the tongue," he continues. "It is a small member but it can make huge claims" (NEB). Only three inches long, yet it can kill a man six feet tall, observes a Japanese proverb.

This little member holds death and life in its power. Proverbs 18:21. It contains equal potentialities for good and evil. Our tongue has the capability to heal or wound, to direct or mislead, to soothe or to burn, to encourage or discourage, to instill confidence or create doubt, to teach good or evil, to bring peace or cause fear, to save a life or to kill. What great power God entrusted to us when He gave us speech! What responsibility!

The godless say, "Our lips are our own: who is lord over us" (Psalm 12:4)? But those who are children of God, born again and indwelt by Christ, acknowledge speech as a gift which they are to use as good stewards to His honor.

Our speech affects others, but it can also affect us. Speech and personality are interactive: to a large extent our personalities determine how we speak, and yet our speech also contributes to the building of our personalities. Each of us is in a sense unique. What we think, the way we do things, and especially what we say and how we say it, determine the kind of "atmosphere" that surrounds us. In the home the parents', but particularly the mother's, personality determines the "temperature and weather conditions" for the family. In the classroom it is the teacher's, in the ward the nurse's. A stranger entering these places is immediately aware of "atmospheric conditions," whether they be fresh or stale, static or calm, warm or cool.

Whenever two or more persons meet, it is impossible to keep the "atmospheres" from contacting and intermingling. Each one may allow himself to be changed by the contributions of those about him, and he, too, is affecting the personalities of others by what he says and does. We can control the elements which we wish to incorporate into our personalities if we are aware of what is happening. But many people are not. Therefore we are stewards of our speech, not only for the sake of our own personalities, but very much also for the sake of those who hear us.

As with all other trusts, we will need to give account of the words we have spoken. In fact, we determine our judgment by our very speech. "For by thy words thou shalt be justified, and by thy words thou shalt be condemned," says Jesus. Matthew 12:37. "There is not a thoughtless [careless, idle] word that comes from men's lips but they will have to account for it on the day of judgment" (NEB), are His preceding words.

Who, then, can be acquitted? For which of us has not said with chagrin when it was too late, "Why did I ever say that? It was so thoughtless, so unnecessary, so unkind"? James tells us what we know to be the truth about ourselves: "All of us often go wrong; the man who never says a wrong thing is a perfect character" (NEB). Who of us qualifies for the "perfect character"? Do we all stand condemned then? We cannot evade the truth.

But let us take heart. Jesus wants so much to help us, to change us, to make us like Himself.

"Come unto me," He invites. "Learn of me."

He will teach us how we should talk as we study His speech

110

and as we talk to Him. He will show us how we can let Him speak through us. Our part is to bring a desire to learn, a willingness to practice the lessons, and a decision to yield our tongues to the lordship of Christ.

We will find that Jesus' words were never destructive flames, nor was His speech ever insipid. But from His lips fell apples of gold, choice silver, gentle rain, and the medicine of life.

A GREAT FIRE

Words can do untold harm when they are not under the control of Christ. They can be as swiftly destructive as fire. The frightening experience of fighting an uncontrolled grass fire once showed us how swift and dangerous such flames can be. In a matter of half an hour the neighbor's unguarded fire had swept through three lots, threatening the destruction of two homes. Apologetically the neighbor explained that she had forgotten to put the screen over the incinerator, and a few sparks had escaped, unnoticed.

In this case the damage was small, but can we ever say the same when a word-fire, sparked by a few gossipy remarks, spreads in all directions? "Gossip travels only a shade slower than electricity," said a radio announcer. James expresses the evil of the tongue in strong language.

"What a huge stack of timber can be set ablaze by the tiniest spark! And the tongue is in effect a fire. It represents among our members the world with all its wickedness; it pollutes our whole being; it keeps the wheel of our existence red-hot, and its flames are fed by hell. Beasts and birds of every kind, creatures that crawl on the ground or swim in the sea, can be subdued and have been subdued by mankind; but no man can subdue the tongue. It is an intractable evil, charged by deadly venom. We use it to sing the praises of our Lord and Father, and we use it to invoke curses upon our fellowmen who are made in God's likeness. Out of the same mouth come praises and curses. My brothers, this should not be so" (James 3:5b-10, NEB).

My neighbor had forgotten the screen. When people forget

to screen their speech with prayer and love, the sparks of gossip, temper, and falsehood can easily fly out and cause untold damage in terms of ruined characters and charred confidences.

Furthermore, the flames are two-directional. They also strike the speaker. Thoughtless and inconsiderate speech causes him unhappiness; gossip often brings the instigator much embarrassment, but more serious, it sullies his soul; breaking confidences causes guilt feelings and remorse; all evil speaking contributes to loss of inner peace. As sound speech helps to build a pleasing personality, so cruel and thoughtless words contribute to inner unwholesomeness. This in turn gives rise to further "corrupt communication." Harsh, thoughtless, cutting words are not only unchristian, but they also show immaturity.

We all enjoy a bit of humor and sharp wit. How many embarrassing situations has it saved, how much tension relieved, how many friendships rescued—when used in the right way at the right time. However, humor is to be sharply distinguished from jesting and sarcasm. Jesting is coarse, worldly, sensual wit. It soils the speaker and the hearers. Sarcasm is speech with a sting. It is meant to hurt, and it does. Only the most qualified may use it as a cleansing agent of another's wrong. In commenting on Ephesians 5:4, J. C. Wenger, in *Separated unto God*, writes:

"Christians ought to be serious-minded, but this does not mean that they cannot enjoy a bit of clean humor occasionally. It is not forbidden in Scripture for the saints to laugh. He who lacks a sense of humor has neither the flexibility of good mental health nor the normal winsomeness of a child of God. . . . Nevertheless it is clear that the inspired apostle is lifting Christians above the calculated exhibition of mental cleverness to a deep Christian gratitude. Christians ought to be a rebuke to the light-mindedness of many moderns."[1]

A bad temper is a vicious flame, even though many people are inclined to deal lightly with it. "We all have to blow off steam sometimes, and an outburst of temper now and then is only normal," they maintain. They are inclined to sym-

112

pathize with the woman who "blew her top" occasionally, perhaps regularly, and explained, "It's only for a few minutes, then it's all over, and I feel better."

"Yes, of course, we understand," was the comment, "it's just like firing a shotgun—one quick loud bang, and then everything is quiet. But what about the damage that has been done?"

Vividly the sight of two children, covering their eyes with their hands and turning away from their mother, comes to mind. It seemed they could not bear the sight of her flashing eyes or the sound of her angry voice. Whenever they did something childish which incited her wrath, they simply shriveled under the scorching tirade, said good-by, and ran out the door. Abruptly one day this Christian mother realized her sin and the possible consequences. In tears she laid the ugliness of it bare before God. He took it away and replaced it with His blessing, which then flowed as healing balm onto her (and His) little ones.

"He that is slow to wrath is of great understanding: but he that is hasty of spirit exalteth folly" (Proverbs 14:29).

The flame of falsehood appears in a variety of forms. There is the matter of half-truths, for example. A certain woman confessed to being caught up in a dilemma which she could not resolve. "Someone will ask me a question which I cannot answer fully because it involves another person, concerning whom I cannot reveal the true facts. And so I give an answer which is truthful as far as it goes, but which I know leaves the questioner with a false impression. Then I feel guilty. Is only part of the truth a falsehood?" What would Christ's solution be, since He is *the* truth?

Flattery is falsehood because it is saying something "that sounds like a compliment when you do not really mean it." Perhaps people resort to flattery because they themselves are insecure and think that saying something nice about a person will put them into his favor. They are using a wrong means to bolster their ego.

Insincerity is another destructive flame. A secular newspaper, in a witty capsule, contains the following definition:

"Tact is making your guests feel at home when you wish they were." We might add that it is telling Judy you are so very glad to see her when you really are not glad at all; or accepting an invitation "with pleasure" when you would much sooner not. How adept many Christian women are at using such "tact"! Though we may succeed in deceiving people, we cannot hide our insincerity from Him who abides in us. To Him it is exactly what it is: lying. Solomon warns, "Lying lips are abomination to the Lord" (Proverbs 12:22). Shall we say then, "Judy, I would rather not be with you," and "I don't feel like accepting your invitation"? That would be the truth. Basically, though, it would be selfishness. The Bible gives no more room for a follower of Jesus to be selfish than to be insincere. We need to re-examine our attitudes. We can be sure that God knows all about our associations in advance, and He has permitted them to happen, or even willed it so. He wants something good to happen to us through each particular experience. (The first good thing is to rid us of any feeling of ill will or superiority.) As soon as we realize God's leading, our confusion is dissolved! We need no longer be insincere in our friendliness. We can only be thankful that God so wisely plans for all details in our lives, and ask Him to make us capable of receiving the blessing He has in store for us. (He may even permit us to be a blessing!)

All of us could probably profit by adopting the New Year's resolution of one woman who wrote, "I resolve, with God's help, to put aside all pretense and be absolutely sincere in all my relationships." This would include not only our spoken words, but also our written ones, our speech via letter writing.

The observation that "some people use language to conceal thought and others instead of thought" simply does not apply to the Christ-controlled person. He is to use language as a God-given gift to express God-inspired thoughts.

Not suiting our actions to our words is inconsistency, and inconsistency is really a lie. If we talk of the power of prayer and pray little; if we extol love and have little, and that mixed with criticism and jealousy; if we refer to God's promises, yet complain and fret and doubt—then our words betray us.

114

Such speech loses even the semblance of power. On the other hand, "truthful lips endure for ever," wrote Solomon (Proverbs 12:19, RSV), and "How forceful are honest words!" said Job (6:25, RSV).

Think of Jesus. Since He is the truth, His words are true. Through all the ages they have not changed: the same yesterday, today, forever. Think of the force behind them: they calmed the storm, they stilled human fears, drove out demons, caused sickness to flee, silenced the enemy, infused His followers with power. He lived the truth.

Speaking and living the truth, that is a life of purity and strength. That is a life of value. "The tongue of the righteous is choice silver" (Proverbs 10:20, RSV).

APPLES OF GOLD

"A word fitly spoken is like apples of gold in a setting of silver" (Proverbs 25:11, RSV). A silver network basket filled with golden-colored apples, or maybe he meant imitation gold apples on silver embroidery. Rich. Precious. Beautiful.

To be fitting, our words must be wisely spoken: "The mind of the wise makes his speech judicious, and adds persuasiveness to his lips" (Proverbs 16:23, RSV). A friend has the following prayer taped above her telephone: "Father in heaven, guide my thoughts. Give me the capacity and willingness to think deeply and to speak thoughtfully. Amen." A fitting prayer, not only for telephone talk, but for every other occasion as well.

Fitting words can act like a tonic. When you feel your spiritual vitality draining, take the vitamins of praise. Read carefully the prescription which is found in Psalm 103. Follow the directions. You will be freed from the complaining which robs you of joy and the faultfinding which causes pain. This tonic must be taken continuously. Our hearts ought to be *occupied* with praising God. "By him [Christ] therefore let us offer the sacrifice of praise to God continually, that is, the fruit of our lips giving thanks to his name" (Hebrews 13:15). It is an act of obedience to make thanksgiving one of the chief aims of our life.

115

Joy is a feeling that does not tolerate restriction. It contains the compulsive element of communication. It might be defined as a feeling of gratitude which must be shared.

"Mother, you're glad about too many things," remarked a little lad smilingly when his mother said that she was glad the flowers were getting a drink from the rain even though she could not hang the clothes out to dry. The next time it rained the boy observed quite cheerfully, even though his friend could not walk over, "Well, anyway, God knows what kind of weather is best." With a little thought, how easily can some of the world's dullness be replaced with cheerfulness, just by remembering to express a little gratitude.

Every, positively every, situation contains some ground for thankfulness, even though it is not always obvious. Could there, for instance, be any element to cause gratitude in such a tragedy as a husband deserting his wife? One woman, having come through the heartbreaking ordeal, was able to say, with trembling lips, "I have lost a great deal, but my spiritual gain has been greater than my loss. I am closer to God than I have ever been in my life. For this I am so thankful."

Surely, if she could say this, and she could not pretend it, then we can find something about which to be thankful when it rains, or when our child is ill, or even when a husband dies. "Rejoice in the Lord alway: and again I say, Rejoice," wrote Spirit-inspired Paul. A Christian woman can do it because Christ is living in her. He spoke of joy in His hour of greatest suffering. There is never a time but we can say, "I am thankful that God's grace is sufficient."

Words can be great healers, acting like medicine on a wound. Did you ever think of the fact that we carry a built-in, fully stocked medicine kit in our mouth? When a little one comes running in with a cut finger, we know where the first-aid supplies are kept, and lose no time in applying the suitable remedy. What about our healing words? When the firecrackers of a quarrel are inflicting painful burns, can we give the "soft answer [that] turneth away wrath"? When the death of a loved one has torn away a portion of the heart, are we skilled in the gentle application of "soothing oint-

116

ment"? When sin has gashed the soul until it is barely recognizable as God's creation, are we able to apply the "balm of Gilead"?

Instantaneous word-healing occurred in the waiting room of a doctor's office one day. Nora, waiting her turn, was sad and weary-looking, yet her face was anxiously tense. It told that she was still fighting, although she knew that she had lost. Then Linda came in. Her face told, not the tale of a battle, but of a victory won, of peace and inner joy. When they had greeted each other, Linda asked gently, "Are you in trouble?"

With a successful effort at self-control Nora revealed the cause of her anxiety: "Mother is dying of cancer and there is no hope."

During the silence that followed Linda struggled to find suitable words of encouragement and sympathy. She waited silently for direction, and then uttered the words which the Spirit gave her, "I wish you much strength for the coming days."

Nora's face broke into a smile and even her eyes lit up. A tiny current of courage was unmistakably beginning to flow again. "Thanks, Linda. Thanks a lot!"

Linda left then, but her healing words continued their therapeutic work. "Anxiety in a man's heart weighs him down, but a good word makes him glad" (Proverbs 12:25, RSV). There are generous supplies of comforting, encouraging, and reconciling words available to those who would follow the divine directions for using them.

Contrary as it may seem, we are sometimes called upon to inflict wounds as well as to heal. Creative criticism has been called the "operation without anesthetic," and it is one of the most difficult to perform. Cutting words, in this sense, are not synonymous with sarcasm or "cutting down to size" with merciless remarks, but are those used to cut away undesirable, harmful, and hindering things in another's character. As Christians we actually have the responsibility to do this within the body of believers. We are all engaged in presenting Christ to the world. If there appears a blemish to spoil this

117

representation, the spot must be removed for His sake. Creative criticism in no way carries the connotation of cruelty, but rather of sympathy. It results in blessing. "Faithful are the wounds of a friend," states the Word. When criticism comes from the heart of love, the wounds will be "faithful" and beneficial. That is how God works.

Constructive criticism is only one form of teaching. Teaching is "to help to know, and to help to grow." Probably more than we think, our speech is utilized in this way. We may be professional schoolteachers, or mothers of young (and not-so-young) children, or the aunt or neighbor lady, or maybe Sunday-school instructors or grandmothers; whatever else we are, we are really all of us teachers, because we help others to know and to grow by our words and actions, whether we realize it or not. Neither is it a matter of choice. It is simply a fact.

If then teachers we must be, let us be good ones. "May my teaching drop as the rain, my speech distil as the dew, as the gentle rain upon the tender grass, and as the showers upon the herb," prays Moses. Deuteronomy 32:2, RSV.

How destructive can a hailstorm or a heavy rain be to a field of young wheat! But when the gentle rain comes, scarcely audible, and the dew, not audible at all, one can almost see the gladness of the tender shoots as they absorb the water and push themselves upward in luscious growth.

Gentle rain—distilled dew—refreshing showers—upon the tender grass. How can our teaching be like that?

Constantly, and probably unconsciously, we are instructing by the example method. When a child surprises us by using some adult expression, we are inclined to ask, "Wherever did he get that?" Obviously, the child heard it from some adult and learned it.

A certain mother, hearing her children scolding each other, asked crossly, "Children, are you quarreling again?"

"Oh, no," came the pleasant reply. "We're only playing 'Mother' !"

Both negative and positive learning can result from following an example. Trying to teach someone to stop shouting

118

by shouting at him is like trying to stop fighting with fighting. By such an example we are teaching what we consider an effective means to stop wrong, namely, more of the same wrong. Besides being altogether faulty, it adds unnecessary noise and pain to the already overabundant supply in the world. On the other hand, how rewarding to hear a child's unsolicited "Thank you" and "I'm sorry," or his pleasant conversation with a guest, or his sympathetic remarks as he helps a younger brother, not because he has been taught these expressions like memorized formulae, but for the most part through unconscious example. Ask the child where he learned these things, and he will truthfully answer, "I don't know."

Much valuable teaching can take place incidentally if we are alert to unscheduled opportunities. An event in nature, a song, or a visit can open the way to real learning.

"We can't exactly make these openings, but we can develop an ear for recognizing them. To reserve such discussion for 'worship time' is to eliminate 95 per cent of our God-given chances to teach, to guide, to shape. And to declare ourselves too busy or too poorly informed to pursue the discussion is to sacrifice the remaining 5 per cent."[2]

And so we teach, not because we have chosen to do so, but because we are women—women, placed in strategic positions, commissioned to use the most effective methods of helping those who come within our sphere of influence. We would do well to take to heart the instructions Paul gives his student-teacher, Titus: "Show yourself in all respects a model of good deeds, and in your teaching show integrity, gravity, and sound speech that cannot be censured" (RSV).

Another area in our lives which does not depend upon choice is witnessing. Everybody witnesses. He witnesses wherever he goes, by his actions, his appearance, and his speech. In these ways he communicates to others whether or not the Lord Jesus means anything to him. The non-Christian says by his way of life, "I don't care about Jesus." The Christian, in varying degrees corresponding to his commitment, says that he loves the Lord. Jesus states that Christians cannot fail to bear witness for Him. Acts 1:8 is not a command, nor is it the final commission of Christ to His disciples. It is simply a statement: "You will receive power when the Holy Spirit comes upon you; and you will bear witness for me . . . to the ends of the earth" (NEB).

Some Christians, unfortunately, harbor the mistaken notion that their good deeds and attractive appearance, necessary as these are, will speak so clearly to their faith that their words of testimony would be superfluous, or even damaging, to their fine living witness. They place the emphasis on action because they have heard it said that "what you do speaks so loudly that I cannot hear what you are saying." Two college girls were practicing this philosophy of witnessing until they were brought sharply to face their real responsibility. A non-Christian asked them angrily, "Why don't you two ever *say* anything? Doesn't your faith mean enough to you even to talk about it? What is there to it anyway?"

The Bible does not support the silent-witness theory.

"Let the redeemed of the Lord say so" (Psalm 107:2).

". . . make the secret plain" (Colossians 4:4, NEB).

". . . be ready always to give an answer to every man that asketh you a reason of the hope that is in you" (I Peter 3:15).

"Go . . . , and tell them how great things the Lord hath done for thee" (Mark 5:19).

Jesus Christ lives in us. He will do the speaking if we only allow Him to. We do not need to "whip up a witness" if we remember His words: "It is not ye that speak, but the Spirit of your Father which speaketh in you" (Matthew 10:20). Even though He is not visible to the human eye, or noticeable in the feelings, He is nonetheless present, always, continuously. He abides. Abiding does not mean visiting, now here and now away. He is unbrokenly with us: "Lo, I am with you alway."

That is the secret to winsome witnessing with words. Jesus used the right approach to all with whom He talked when He was on earth in human form, and He does the same today through His followers. To the measure that we are conscious of His presence, praying for His guidance, following

His directions, we will be successful witnesses for Him. It might be to a member of our family, to a neighbor, a co-worker, a student, or a patient. It might be to a caller at the door or a fellow traveler. It might be anybody in this whole wide world. Think of the absolutely wonderful privilege of having Jesus Christ speak to them through us!

Gladys Aylward gives a vivid account of how she unexpectedly came to the point of consecrating her gift of speech to God. Her testimony appears in a booklet, "My Story and Testimony," presented by *Sunday Companion*. She remembers how, when she felt God calling her to go to China, she told her father that she would like to go to this country. Her father, a silent sort of man, just asked her what she intended to do there. When she answered that she did not know, he reminded her that she was not a nurse or a teacher, and so couldn't nurse or teach anyone, to which she had to agree. Swinging suddenly around, he looked hard at her and said, "Oh, go on, get out! All you can do is talk!"

She went outside the kitchen door into the hallway and wept. Her father didn't understand, bless him! she told herself, because the Lord had not called him. But He had definitely called her. Then the wonderful thought struck her that what her father had said was true: she could talk.

"All right, then—" she told the Lord, "I'll talk, and I'll talk, and I'll talk, and I'll talk. I'll just keep on talking, but it will be all for you."

From that very moment God put words into her mouth and she testifies that she has "talked solidly ever since," and a great deal of it in a language foreign to her own.

Heaven alone will reveal how many people are there because of the help of this missionary's testimony: an ordinary woman, and yet so extraordinary because she is allowing God to speak through her.

"And now, Lord, . . . grant unto thy servants, that with all boldness they may speak thy word," prayed the disciples (Acts 4:29), and Paul testifies, as though in response, "My speech and my message were . . . in demonstration of the Spirit and power" (I Corinthians 2:4, RSV).

121

There is, indeed, a time to speak, but there is also a time not to speak. To be able to discern rightly between the two is a mark of wisdom.

How talkative people are! Except for the person who has inherited reticent speech tendencies and the rare golden specimen who has learned to listen, our world is full of people who love to talk. With most persons one does not need to worry about conversational lags. A question will set them talking, and a comment now and again will keep them going.

How much of all this talk is really necessary? Does it show a lack of knowledge, a shallowness of understanding? "He that hath knowledge spareth his words," wrote Solomon. Proverbs 17:27. To carry the point farther, how much is actually harmful, and therefore evil? It is claimed that 90 per cent of the world's sufferings come from words.

God, through the Scriptures, admonishes us time after time to restrain our tongues. For our own protection and well-being as well as that of others, we ought to be careful not to talk too much. The writer of Proverbs counsels: "Whoso keepeth his mouth and his tongue keepeth his soul from troubles," and "He that keepeth his mouth keepeth his life: but he that openeth wide his lips shall have destruction."

A weary mother sank into the rocking chair when at last the children were in bed. In her reflection on the noisy events of the day she came to the stark conclusion that she herself had contributed much to causing the undesirable noises that had made her so tired. She had scolded instead of helping, which resulted in crying. She had called loudly when a few steps would have brought her within whispering distance. She had repeated directions when she should have allowed the children the responsibility of obeying at the first request. She had talked and talked when a smile could have said it all.

How often the noisy house or classroom is the result of our talking too much too loudly: a real energy drainer. We are like the little boat that could, and did, toot very loudly and very long. But every time it tooted, it had to stop. Feature its progress.

122

Scripture counsels: "Study to be quiet."

We pray: "Lord, help me to talk less and to say more."

Better than to be able to speak ten languages is to learn to keep quiet in one! Silence, besides offering the world a refreshingly quiet pause, is our opportunity to learn, to appreciate, to grow, to become rich!

"I used to think, secretly," tells an acquaintance, "that I was the most clever one in the Bible discussion group. My ideas were the best ones, naturally, and I lost no time in making them known. Nobody else ever said very much anyway. (How could they when I had already said everything worth mentioning?) Then I went away for a while and through a painful process of self-examination learned something. When I returned to my study group I was a little less voluble. The solutions to problems did not come prefabricated as they used to. The others had begun to voice their opinions. In my absence they had discovered that they *could* quite nicely get along without me. Repeatedly it has happened that someone will clearly put into words what is being hazily formed in my mind. How that thrills me! It proves our unity in the Lord. He is giving both of us His thoughts. Now before I speak I try to remember to ask God if He really wants me to speak or if He would rather I be silent for a while."

We ask for God's guidance in our speech. Let us add another request: guidance for silence.

SPEECH WITHOUT WORDS

There is a language that does not employ words, and yet it is clearly understood, even by an infant. It is the language of tone, look, gesture, and laughter.

A very common remark can take on a variety of meanings depending on the tone in which it is offered. Try the phrase, "Imagine that!" With different emphasis of tone it can be an expression of wonder, surprise, disgust, sarcasm, anger, indifference, or delight. Sometimes the tone can initiate a long chain of reaction. The tone in which, for instance, we call someone's name will determine the attitude with which that person will respond to our call. His attitude determines his receptivity to what we have to say to him. This in turn helps determine his further action in relation to us and to others. As our hearts are "tuned in" to Jesus Christ, the tones of our voices will be in harmony with His love.

The look can speak volumes without a word being uttered. Silent messages are constantly being transmitted by the eyes and facial expressions.

When little Edward, who had been playing in the coalbin, remarked casually to his mother that she would probably have to wash his pants and shirt, she did not say a word, but went on with her work. Unable to endure the silence, the boy ventured cautiously, holding his hands over his face, "I'm not going to look at you. The way you look doesn't make me very happy."

Not a syllable of reproach had been uttered, but the message had been clearly conveyed.

An observant youngster was quite free with his compliment: "Daddy, you have trees around your eyes when you smile—old, dried-up trees, without any leaves. I like them."

All people smile in the same language. The genuine smile emerges through the eyes, sometimes bypassing the lips. It has been observed that to little children it is the eyes that reveal personality. No matter how unattractive the face, if the eyes speak the language of love and kindness, the child is drawn to the person. If they do not, regardless of beauty, the child is not attracted to him. This response probably applies to people of all ages.

The Christian woman has it in the power of her look to draw others to the attractive Christ.

Gestures speak. A shrug of the shoulders can say, "I don't know," or "I don't care," depending on the angle of the eyebrows and the set of the mouth. A stamping foot says angry things; a hearty handclasp conveys friendly greetings. A hand on the shoulder speaks support and encouragement. A shaking index finger scolds, and a beckoning hand calls. Have we ever thought of applying Colossians 3:23 to our gestures: "Whatsoever ye *do*, do it heartily, as to the Lord"? That

124

would exclude any gesture which transmits a message other than Christian love.

Then there is the language of laughter. What's in a laugh? Often people laugh because they think something is funny. But sometimes they laugh for other reasons. Sometimes their thoughts are transmitted better that way than by words. Sometimes they do not know what to say, and so they laugh because they are nervous. And sometimes they laugh because they are hurt.

How well do we understand this language? A mother understands it. When her daughter unburdens the pain of her heart and laughs during the telling, the mother will say, "I know why you are laughing. It is because you do not want to cry." Is our perception that fine?

Have we learned to communicate in this language? June has. An anxious woman asked her confidentially, "Has it ever occurred to you that there is something wrong with me, with my mind, I mean?" June's response consisted simply of an open, hearty, happy laugh. It wiped the tension off the anxious woman's face and replaced it with a smile which broke into a laugh of thanks. Volumes spoken, yet no words employed.

Are we sensitive enough to know the difference between laughing with someone and at him? Are we big enough never to indulge in the latter, whether the person will ever know or not?

A woman's highest possible desire is that her heart be so filled with Christ Himself that His love can come to expression in all her speech, spoken or unspoken. Those who consciously and persistently (and penitentially upon failure) practice His presence will receive the well-done reward, "Thou good and faithful servant: thou hast been faithful over the gift of speech which I entrusted to thee."

About the Writer

Mary Pankratz Rempel (Mrs. Dietrich) was born in Saskatchewan, Canada, and spent her early childhood on the prairies. When she was ten, the family moved to Mission City, British Columbia, where the mountains often echoed with the shouts and laughter of the ten children who could form their own softball team or strawberry-picking squad. After teacher training at Vancouver Normal School, she taught for seven years in British Columbia elementary schools. She has written primary Sunday-school lessons and edited *Unser Missionsblatt,* the German missions paper of the Canadian Women's Conference, for three years. She now lives with her husband and three children, Harvey, Nadine, and Nelda, in North Newton, Kansas, where her husband serves as Sunday-school secretary for the General Conference Mennonite Church.

FOOTNOTES

1. John C. Wenger, *Separated unto God* (Scottdale, Pa.: Mennonite Publishing House), p. 97.
2. Elaine Sommers Rich (Ed.), *Breaking Bread Together* (Scottdale, Pa.: Herald Press), p. 348.

Quotations with "NEB" are from the *New English Bible,* © The Delegates of the Oxford University Press and the Syndics of the Cambridge University Press 1961.

WHERE *there is hatred, let me sow love;*
Where there is injury, pardon;
Where there is doubt, faith;
Where there is despair, hope;
Where there is darkness, light;
Where there is sadness, joy.

Oh, divine master, grant that I may not so much seek
To be consoled, as to console;
To be understood, as to understand;
To be loved, as to love.
For it is in giving that we receive;
It is in pardoning that we are pardoned;
It is in dying that we are born to eternal life.
Lord, make me an instrument of thy peace. Amen.

                                   —*St. Francis of Assisi.*

8

STEWARDSHIP OF TALENTS
AND ABILITIES

LOIS BARTEL

THE man in the Parable of the Talents who hid all his money was not praised for his caution! If Christ was referring only to money when He gave this illustration, many of us can forget about it, since we have little money to bury. But the parable catches us too. Christ wasn't as concerned about money as He was about the servants. The talents He told about symbolize our abilities and our natural gifts. Talents such as the ability to sing a solo or to paint a picture are included, but equally important are the small talents which, when added together and used properly, actually become the most dynamic. If we are not stewards of these, their potential will be lost.

What does it mean to be a steward? It implies being included in the management of God's estate. We become God's stewards immediately after we become His children. Knowing that we are God's stewards it is inconsistent to believe we own anything, for He owns us. Do you think it selfish of God to claim ultimate ownership of all we possess?

God did not institute stewardship for His own sake. Writes Milo Kauffman: "It cannot be too strongly emphasized that God's purpose in the stewardship of man is for the good of man. Christian stewardship inevitably will result in enrichment of life. The greatest value of Christian stewardship is what it does for the individual. When Jesus told the rich young ruler to sell what he had and give to the poor, it was not the money that Jesus was especially interested in—it was the young man. It was the rich ruler that Jesus loved, not his possessions. God asks man to be a good steward because of what it will do for man.[1]

"Christian stewardship frees man from the tyranny of things, and helps him to a life of freedom and joy through the contribution of self, time, talents, and money to the advancement of the kingdom of Christ.[2] . . . Christian stewardship helps make God real to man. Thinking of God as the owner of our lives, our time, our talent, and our possessions helps us think of Him as a living personality."

To be God's stewards we must first know what we are to be stewards of. Of course we are stewards of all God has given us: love, good health, good family, good friends, good home, good looks, education, talent, influence, social leadership, popularity, business ability, wages, income, material possessions.

And yet, is not each of us responsible to find and use these talents? This requires utmost honesty. Yet it is necessary. "What if I do with ardor what a thousand could, maybe, and leave undone forever what was only meant for me?"[3]

Let us explore the areas where our abilities and talents become apparent and can be put to use.

KNOW THYSELF

We will begin closest home and examine the "self." Unless one's personal "house" is examined there is not much point in reaching beyond. "The unexamined life is not worth living. . . . Know thyself" (Socrates). May we add, know thy powers? When we realize the powers and abilities in us, we will have incentive to use them.

All too often feelings of incompetence keep us from venturing out in areas in which we do not feel secure. Why do we let feelings of incompetence limit us? Where would Helen Keller be if she had said, "I can't"?

Is it not an insult to our Creator if we don't even recognize the gifts He gives us? If we sincerely believe we are made in

God's image, we are bound to find strength and ability. Is our God too small or can we let Him use His creativity, by letting it flow through us?

Martin Buber, contemporary Israeli philosopher, says this regarding recognizing and using our powers: "Every person born into this world represents something new, something that never existed before, something original and unique. It is the duty of every person to know . . . that there has never been anyone like him in the world, for if there had been someone like him, there would have been no need for him to be in the world. Every single man is a new thing in the world and is called upon to fulfill his particularity in this world."[4]

Psychologists tell us that we each have a strong tendency to become that which we imagine ourselves to be. William Cranmer, former administrator at Boys Village, Smithville, Ohio, operated his treatment center for delinquent boys under the philosophy that the boys would become what the staff expected them to become. Expectations! "If God be for us, who can be against us?" "All things are possible to him that believeth." If we truly believe this, faith in our own powers will grow. Faith will emerge which releases forces which will be invaluable to us.

We need to know in what areas we personally have the most power. It is necessary that we recognize our abilities honestly. God has given out an assortment of gifts. To some He has given spare time, to others a surplus of physical or mental energy, or a special art or skill. To others He has given ideas, imagination, ability to organize, or to lead. God expects us to recognize that we have something that will contribute to others and He expects us to use it. It may be a spectacular soprano voice, or it may be a soft, appropriately spoken word. It may be the ability to be the chairman of a large organization or it may be helping to organize a small committee. Either is important. Remember, "Unto whomsoever much is given, of him shall be much required" (Luke 12:48b).

If we become convinced that we must put ourselves to use, the results may surprise us. It may make us appear

131

different. It may make us break with ways of doing things which are considered the "only way," but Paul speaks reassuringly to this. It shouldn't matter, he says. "Don't let the world fit you into its own mold."

BE MENTALLY AWAKE

To be alert to areas in which we can effectively serve we must be mentally awake. Awareness of the world makes us more interesting persons and makes it easier to relate to others. It helps us utilize God-given intelligence. One need not sit in a classroom to get an education. One splendid opportunity to learn more about any subject desired is through books. They offer entertainment and fascination as well as education. Books can help us discover who we are.

They open many doors. A woman should not feel guilty for sitting down to read them if her time is well budgeted.

"What powers God has entrusted to us in giving us our minds! He has given us powers of reason, judgment, imagination, memory; power to invent, to plan and execute, to have dominion over His creation; power to build, or to destroy; power to dominate, or power to serve."[5]

By learning how to think clearly and orderly and how to utilize our intelligence we spawn creative ideas. We should learn to trust our own minds. It is easier to do this when our intellectual abilities are well nourished. "To be creative means to experience life in one's own way, to perceive from one's own person, to draw upon one's own resources, capacities, roots. In each of us lies that spark of divine spirit that fulfills itself only when we establish contact with our Creator, only when we find a central core from which to gear our everyday moments. In each of us lies a part of the Creator Himself; and if we fail to utilize our capacity for creative expression, we necessarily limit God, for it is we who are stewards of that which is within us. If this be true, then why, if each of us has the potential to live more creatively, are we always in need of the few who will accept responsibility for themselves, for their time, for their talents?"[6]

132

Knowing and using our personal abilities will produce unbelievable results. The things we do and the way we act should be under the complete guidance of God, so that the very way we live reveals something of His goodness and love. If we are to utilize God's gifts to us, we must have His guidance. The center of one's life permeates the whole. If God is at the center, He will be with us in our whole life. From our communication (prayer) unending energy will be generated.

When one matures in his Christian life, he becomes concerned less with self and more with others. Likewise, when our lives as stewards mature and when we become more acquainted with and confident of our potential, our thoughts can then turn toward others. We will be concerned with what we are able to do for them. It is when we are comfortable with ourselves (although not necessarily satisfied) that we look beyond and help others.

Christian stewardship will help to solve our personal problems. We will no longer feel frustrated and useless. We will see a purpose in life if we know that we are God's and we are working together with Him in His world.

AT HOME

What talents in this area can we find and use? Our first outreach is in the home.

An infant gets his first and most lasting impression of the world from his mother and her feelings. A woman can "make" or "break" her husband's future. These facts point out the important role of a woman in the home. Think of the far-reaching implications!

My teaching experience called this to my attention. On enrollment day it was our policy to ask the mothers about their occupation. When asked this question one mother looked sheepish and then with some embarrassment answered, "Oh, I'm just a housewife." Inwardly I rebelled. Yes, I thought, you are just a housewife. All you are is a wife, mother, companion, counselor, cook, dietitian, teacher, laun-

133

dress, cleaning lady, medical director, financial director, and spiritual leader. That's all.

What woman has not been asked by some well-meaning person, "Are you working?" Naturally, what he really means is, Do you have some job outside your home which brings in money? But that is not what he implies. The original question implies that if a woman does not have an outside job she is not working. No wonder housewives resent the questions.

Too often the job of being a housewife is thought of as a period of intellectual stagnation. This need not be so. Opportunities for creativity are endless. One needs only to watch and to observe a day in the life of a mother to see how wide her scope of knowledge and understanding must be. This is one of the few remaining free professions—where the woman is permitted to organize her own responsibilities and activities.

True, the demands of the kitchen, nursery, and home can be staggering and discouraging at times. But if work is truly "love made visible," cleaning mud off the floor or washing smudges from windows may not seem so disgusting. Much depends on our mental attitudes toward our lot. Housecleaning can seem as futile as stringing beads on a rope without a knot at the end, or it can be a time in which our thoughts can take us to new heights. It is amazing how far a mind can wander from the dustcloth, dishpan, or diaper pail.

A woman needs to employ all her abilities to tackle this vocation. She needs to be the stable center around which the household revolves. She provides a conducive atmosphere for mental, spiritual, emotional, and physical growth.

For her husband this means what it did to Mina in *Come Spring*. She felt she was the root and her husband the tree. She was the ground out of which he grew. She felt her job was to be good growing ground so that her husband would succeed.[7]

Many women get sufficient satisfaction from the daily task of food preparation and do an excellent job of it. Cooking can be a challenging area. Elizabeth Yates writes, "It is a

134

tool of living, and excellent results can be obtained with so little money if you care enough."[8]

Short cuts and original ideas made by each housewife are most effective. One method used to get out of a rut in meal planning is to tear appealing recipes and pictures out of magazines when reading and to paste them in a 15-cent scrapbook. At a later time, paging through, the pictures will attract the eye and the recipe will liven up a meal. When a recipe proves itself, it can be placed in a permanent file box.

To women who find the den more attractive than the kitchen, justification can be made for "buying one hour of time," as one advertising agency puts it, by buying a "mix."

Do we see our job as that of a housewife or homemaker? A seventh grade class was asked the difference between a house and a home—a housewife and a homemaker. One girl said a housewife is "just a person cleaning the house. A homemaker does not only keep house, but keeps and makes it a pleasant place to live." What a challenge to homemakers!

COMMUNITY

A woman can hardly be completely effective in her personal life and in the home without having contacts in the community. If stewardship means partnership with God, our concern will reach out beyond ourselves and our family.

How can this happen? E. Stanley Jones says, "It cannot be insisted too much that abundant living means abundant giving. . . . Just as you would smother yourself to death if you only breathed in and refused to breathe out, so if you are not outgoing, the whole process of incoming will stop, and you will die spiritually, mentally, and physically. If a cow is not milked, it will go dry. If you are not giving out to others, you, too, will go dry in spirit."[9]

One area, volunteer work for service in hospitals, homes, and such places, is sometimes hampered because people with potential ability do not know where they can be useful. Also they do not realize that the greatest gift they can give shut-ins is to know them as individuals and let the shut-ins show respect and response.

135

Often, however, the most effective opportunity to serve comes at the least expected time and in the most unspectacular way. In dealing with others, little things mean a lot. Longfellow once said, "Give what you have. To someone it may be better than you dare to think."[10]

Dunn claims that in giving oneself to others one is more effective when he follows warmhearted impulses than when he follows well-planned, calculated actions.[11] We never know when such an action will have great meaning to a friend or neighbor. One example would be offering a lift to a lady loaded down with parcels, before we reason that she probably lives just around the corner. Another would be complimenting a waitress on service before we have time to reason that she is only doing a job for which she will be paid.

Seldom do we realize that, in giving to others, things as small as minutes are appreciated. Have you not appreciated it when someone took the time to notice your dress and comment on it? Or, is it not meaningful when someone notices a plant you have been "babying"? Receiving a card or note from a friend when going through one of life's joys or sorrows is nice, but is it not particularly touching to hear from someone from whom you had not expected a word? Perhaps an act taking a minimum of time will have a monumental effect.

But this is not easy! We are hindered by two very common things in our society. First, usually we wait until it is too late—an "easy out." Second, what will others think? Will they think I'm just trying to get in good? Will my motives be mistaken? Josephine Benton in *Pace of a Hen* asks, "Why is it we are so afraid of being kind? We fear being classed as Lady Bountifuls or Do-gooders; we fear a psychological analysis of our motives; we fear we are rationalizing some manifestation of ego. All motives are mixed. We can only offer our motives to God, saying humbly, 'I know that this deed will give me satisfaction; I know that if I were my neighbor I would appreciate his coming to see me; I know that our Lord told us we were His disciples if we loved and served one another. Take my motives, Lord, and use them for Thy glory and the welfare of all Thy children.' "[12]

Giving will bear fruit if the spirit in which we give is friendly, if we pick the appropriate time for it, and if we are sincere and enthusiastic.

The greatest thing one can do for another, however, is to pray for him. Does God depend on this labor of love? Writes Benton, "Apparently there are some gifts which God chooses to give through love's labor and planning and prayer. . . . We must not fail those whose weal depends upon our toil and thought—and prayer."[13]

Stephen Grellet puts the challenge of using one's abilities in the community this way: "I expect to pass through this world but once. Any good therefore that I can do, or any kindness that I can show to any fellow creature, let me do it now. Let me not defer or neglect it, for I shall not pass this way again."[14]

CHURCH

The visible church could not exist unless people were willing to contribute their talents and abilities. Such actions not only strengthen the church but also the individual involved. Working and praying together will bind Christ's church closer to Him. Joseph Murray writes, "The more you do, the more you will be asked to do. That is the blessed penalty for willingness. The more you do, the more you will be able to do. That is the blessed law of effort. The more you do, the more it will mean to you. That is the blessed promise of reward in the Master's service. They know Him best who serve Him most."[15]

Those serving in the church program should never do it as a duty, but because they want to serve God. In a Sunday morning message, Victor Sawatsky referred to the Parable of the Talents. He compared the hiding of the talents to the individual who refuses to take any office in the church because he is afraid of becoming involved. The key word, he said, is "afraid." This individual will not teach a class because he is afraid of making mistakes and of having people laugh at him. He is afraid of saying the wrong thing and offending someone. He is afraid of opposition in any office. In other words, he is afraid to take upon himself the self-discipline which is involved in holding any office in church.

Love for Christ, Victor Sawatsky continued, is the highest motive for service and the greatest force for faithfulness. He concluded, "We should give our best talent to the office, however small it may be. May we give of ourselves in living service to Christ and overcome our fear of becoming involved."

CONTINUED GROWTH

We have looked at the major areas of our lives and how we as Christian stewards can contribute our talents and abilities that God has given us. Since we have been made in the image of our Creator, we too should be creating—not only art and music, but also joy, understanding, and love. A mature steward will change privileges into responsibilities. May our prayer be that God will guide us to a life of greater stewardship of the abilities He has given us.

About the Writer

Lois Franz Bartel (Mrs. Gladwin) was born and reared in eastern Washington state. She attended Bethel College, North Newton, Kansas, where she met her husband, Gladwin, and where she received an A.B. degree in social science. She and her husband spent two years in Smithville, Ohio, in MCC Voluntary Service, working with delinquent boys. She also taught sixth grade two years in Halstead, Kansas. Today her husband is doing postgraduate work at the University of Wisconsin, and Lois is engaged in homemaking for him and their young son, Baron Craig, born in 1962.

138

FOOTNOTES

1. Milo Kauffman, *The Challenge of Christian Stewardship* (Scottdale, Pa.: Herald Press, 1955), p. 167.
2. *Ibid.*, p. 157.
3. *Ibid.*
4. Buber, *Hasidism and Modern Man*, Ed. and translated by Maurice Friedman (New York: Horizon Press, 1958), p. 139.
5. Kauffman, *op. cit.*, p. 34.
6. General Conference *Mission Study Guide*, p. 45.
7. Josephine Moffett Benton, *The Pace of a Hen* (Philadelphia: Christian Education Press, 1961), p. 13.
8. Elizabeth Yates, "Pebble in a Pool," *Christian Living* (August, 1962), p. 2.
9. Kauffman, *op. cit.*, p. 158.
10. David Dunn, *Try Giving Yourself Away* (Prentice-Hall, 1956), p. 11.
11. *Ibid.*, p. 13.
12. Benton, *op. cit.*, p. 80.
13. *Ibid.*, p. 97.
14. Dunn, *op. cit.*, p. 106.
15. Joseph J. Murray, *A Faith for Youth*, G.C. Sunday School Quarterly, April to June, 1962, p. 99.
Special thanks go to my sisters in Washington, South Dakota, New York, and Kansas for sharing their talents and abilities by offering their help and suggestions.

PARADOX OF LIFE

Living is being born,
Rising from nothing
Into a body
Of reacting emotions.

Living is bearing,
sharing,
lifting,
breaking,
cleaving,
and forsaking.

And living is dying,
Putting away the empty shell.
Living is dying—
To live again![1]
   —M. Elizabeth Gehman.

9

STEWARDSHIP OF HEALTH AND SUFFERING

EVELYN BAUER

GIFT OF GOD: A JOURNEY OF LIFE

To EACH person born is given a journey of life by the Creator. Ahead of each newly born infant stretch the possibilities of self-determination—youth and vigor, health to use and spend, waning health, old age and death. A whole life process, whether long or short, is given to each individual.

We who have matured beyond the first stages of life cannot predict how much longer our journey will be. Termination of life is not meant to be in our hands. But what we do with our health does affect our length of life.

Stewardship of health is a rather new term. We hear more frequently about stewardship of time, abilities, and material possessions. We are stewards of all of life; our health is an essential part of life. If we wish to say "thank you" to God for life, we will want to be good stewards of our measure of health. How can we do this? There are no easy answers. As in other areas it is not so much a choice between good and bad as between several goods.

We need to search for life's meaning, frame it, and hold it up before us for viewing. "Why are we here?" After we answer this ageless question for ourselves, life has direction and purpose.

Dr. Henry Hitt Crane, a Methodist minister, discussed this

problem in a Goshen College chapel service. He said that the goal of many people in life is health, wealth, and happiness. But after a time of striving for these values, they find there is a contradiction, "a peculiar antagonism," in this triad which make them cancel each other. In running after happiness, health may suffer. In working for wealth, both health and happiness may be lost. The struggle is futile.

Two extreme reactions have resulted. One is asceticism. Some people try to escape the vicious cycle by withdrawing from life. They embrace vows of chastity, poverty, or namelessness. The opposite reaction appears more frequently—that of "live it up." People try to get out of life what they can, gratify the senses, and accumulate money by hook or by crook.

Along comes life interpreted by high, ethical religion, explained Dr. Crane, and it says life on earth is a transitional experience, not an end in itself. A graphic way to look at why we are here uses the analogy of the womb.

Nine months of prenatal life are required for the creating of a physical entity. A physical body is formed which will be able to support itself, grow and develop after shedding its shell at birth.

Nine hundred months (more or less) of postnatal life are for the creating of a spiritual entity. Our mature physical bodies are to be used for the developing of a soul, a spiritual personality or being, which will live on after shedding the physical body in death.

Our life here is concerned with this second life process or stage—learning about our relationship with God. The greatest satisfaction known to mankind is found in some form of creativity. All of us have the opportunity and capacity to create something of ourselves for the glory of God. We are commanded to glorify God in the *body* as well as in the spirit. I Corinthians 6:20. Jesus gives us power to grow and develop our infinite resources. Life as a transitional experience in this context has profound meaning.

The physical body as the womb of the soul has a high station. Paul expressed this clearly when he said our bodies are

142

temples of the Holy Spirit. The Christian attitude toward the body is different from that of other religions. Pagans abuse and try to punish their bodies. Christians revere them as the dwelling place of the great God.

The Bible reminds us that we were bought with a price. When we use someone else's automobile, camera, or lawn mower, we try to take better care of it than we would if it were our own. We must treat our bodies with the care and respect due to another's property, writes J. Carter Swain, in his book, *Body, Soul, and Spirit*. Most of what we are and have was bought with a price, paid by others. Our mothers suffered to bring us to birth, family and friends paid for our education, and most of us owe our lives or health to medical knowledge and skill, all of which cost someone else something. Even on a secular level, how can we say, "It's my life and I can do what I want with it"?

This body of ours is no mean temple. When we consider how wonderfully it is made, a feeling of awe grips us. Speaking of just one part of the body, Charles M. Crowe wrote in *Stewardship Sermons*:

"Take the human brain, the seat of human thought and action. The few ounces of matter in our skulls and spinal cords do the work continually of 1,000 telephone switchboards, each big enough to serve a city the size of New York. The brain has 140,000,000 neurons. These have the incredible ability to hook together thousands of circuits in the fraction of a second to make possible our thoughts, learning, and decisions. At the same time our 'little brain,' the cerebellum, is continually seeing to it that 750 muscles of the body automatically are tensed and relaxed by exactly the right amount at exactly the right time."[2]

We cannot take lightly the uses to which we put our bodies. They are machines which can wear out. Wrong uses of the body—perversion of sex, gluttony, bondage to tobacco and alcohol, vain manipulations for the sake of pride—must be avoided, not only for physical health reasons, but for the deeper reason that the body, sacred as a church, is not to be desecrated. She who keeps this in mind is better prepared to appreciate God's provision for developing our souls that will live on after the body has served its purpose.

Like time, talents, and money, good health is expendable. Not only is it something to preserve; it is to be used—given to certain causes and investments. Jesus gave us a fine example in giving His life a ransom for many. His life was not long in years, but it served the purpose for which it was given. Christ died for us; we can live for Him with whatever health and length of days we are given. A day of accounting comes to all: ". . . that every one may receive the things done *in his body*, according to that he hath done, whether . . . good or bad" (II Corinthians 5:10).

THE GIFT OF GOOD HEALTH, VIGOR, STRENGTH

In our journey of life the period between childhood and old age is the time known as that of life's greatest usefulness. This section of life, however, may not be the most important in God's sight, even though it is the time of greatest physical activity. Each section of our life journey has its special gifts from God.

What does a Christian woman do with her time of greatest vigor? She may raise and care for a family, or she may pursue a career which contributes to the welfare of mankind in other ways. As she spends her days, she takes a certain attitude toward her own personal gift of health, either consciously or unconsciously.

Two extremes are quite common, and both are improper outlooks. The first is not taking enough care of one's health, and the other is too much concern over minor or imagined health problems. While squandering health on trivialities, or knowingly ruining health, is more than foolishness, one can go to the other extreme and become a self-centered neurotic, pampering one's health. Both of these shorten or negate a person's usefulness to others. Such people are poor stewards of their measure of health.

Christ's call to us is to live for Him, to spend our lives, not waste them. The hypochondriac quite literally loses her life by trying to save it. Even though her physical health might

144

be nearly perfect to begin with, she loses her mental, emotional, and spiritual health, and these in turn may affect the physical.

Dr. Paul Tournier, a contemporary Swiss psychiatrist, in a careful study of what the Bible teaches about the meaning of life, found that scarcely any distinction is made in the Scriptures between organic and inorganic things, between biological and spiritual life. Life is a force which comes from God, animating all living beings. This same force—the Spirit —gives man his moral conscience and wakes in him what we call his spiritual life.

God has placed in every biological being, in every live cell, a regulator to govern it, a plan for it to live by. There is for each organism a certain margin of normal oscillation, but the automatic pilot corrects deviations and keeps it on course. Disease is an oscillation beyond the normal margin. Death is the loss of the regulator. God has a will, a purpose behind the whole plan.

Like biological life, spiritual life does not follow a straight line. It too is made up of perpetual oscillations, but has its regulator, the voice of God in the conscience. Doubt and temptation are normal oscillations. A more violent one is disobedience to God—sin—which brings the regulator into action, calling us back to faith and obedience through confession and forgiveness. This perpetual rediscovery of our relationship to God, with its new understanding of His will, is the meaning of life, says Dr. Tournier.

God's guidance does not preserve us from errors of direction, but these very errors help us to know God better. Such a life which is open to God's guidance has significance and is the only truly happy life. Doctors Tournier and Crane would agree that learning to know God is the key purpose and great opportunity which this life in the physical body affords.

What then does all this have to do with stewardship of health? It reminds us that physical, mental, and spiritual health are intertwined. Health is wholeness and its first requirement is to live purposefully. As an illustration we can note that many outstanding missionaries lived long lives, far

145

out of proportion to the numerous hazards and dangers they had encountered—John G. Paton, Mary Slessor, Dr. Ida Scudder, Dr. Albert Schweitzer, to name a few.

When we are busy living for Christ, we may be called upon to *spend* our health in the so-called prime of life.

Mandombe, one of the first converts in the Congo, had seen many of his people, including his wife, die of sleeping sickness. When medical missionaries determined to find a cure for this disease, they found they would need a human guinea pig. Mandombe willingly volunteered himself, even to be sent to what was the other end of the world for him, England, where, having contracted the disease, he could be studied.

When he was very ill and about to die, doctors asked him if he would not like to return to his country. Being among one's own people at the time of death is important to the Congolese. Mandombe with weakened voice asked if the doctors had finished their discoveries. They said, "No, not yet, but we are now on the right track." Mandombe replied, "Keep on. I will stay." Could we say this dedicated Christian was not a good steward of his health?

Also there was Madeleine Barot. At the end of World War II, she and three other healthy young people went into prison camps in France and asked to live, eat, and sleep like those interned. They felt they could best learn how to correct hopeless situations by firsthand experience of the bad conditions. Their sacrifices led to the beginning of the CIMADE organization. Were they not good stewards of their gifts of youthful health and vigor?

These persons risked their health, but purposely, not by squandering it on trivialities or selfish pursuits. Frances Schervier prayed over a hundred years ago: "What is mine through Thy gift, let it be Thine through my gift."

Most of us are not called upon to take such great risks. So we must concentrate on how we can preserve and make more useful God's gifts of health to us. If someone presents us with a material gift out of a great love for us, we would completely nullify our gratitude if we proceeded to take no care whatever of the gift and caused it to become ugly or useless by abuse. God's gifts need to be cherished.

How then should we look at physical health, one facet of our whole well-being? Modern woman is blessed with new physical health which was not available to women in the years before medical science blossomed. Her new status brings new responsibilities as well as new problems. Christ was greatly concerned with physical healing when He lived as a man upon earth. We believe today's great strides in medicine are a continuation of His ministry through the minds and hands of men. He promised that those coming after Him would do greater works than He. Healing the body is a part of His work which men today, in the medical profession, have continued with divine blessing.

With medical help available we would be foolish to ignore the advice and treatment of trained physicians. As Christian stewards we need to avail ourselves of the scientific knowledge helpful for maintaining good health. The body requires nutritious food, sufficient water, exercise, and rest. Those whose daily work is chiefly sedentary need periods of exercise in harmony with their age and stamina. Rest is necessary to restore physical energy. Recreation, which is closely related to rest, may simply mean a change in activity. In our day of overemphasis on leisure, we need to guard against a laziness in the name of rest and recreation which detracts from our Christian usefulness. But we must provide enough of both to maintain health and a fruitful ministry. The body must be kept in good condition and also kept in subjection.

Two diseases which cause many deaths in the United States are heart disease and cancer. The former can be guarded against by exerting self-control in eating. To keep from becoming overweight in a land of plenty is not easy. It may not be necessary for all of us to count calories, but we can profitably cut down on rich, fatty foods. Following medical advice for early detection of cancer and other diseases which are curable when discovered in their early stages may be a Christian responsibility.

147

More than is usually realized, there is a definite connection between physical health and spiritual vitality. The well-known missionary author, Isobel Kuhn, related in her book, *In the Arena,* how she had looked forward to spending rich hours in prayer during a stay in a hospital. But when the time came, she found that her weakened physical condition made it impossible for her to participate in the intercessory prayer she had hoped to do. At first she became alarmed. She wondered what was wrong with herself, whether she was backsliding. Then she saw that to pray for others as she was accustomed required *physical* as well as spiritual strength. She had no physical strength with which to rally her forces of mental concentration needed for this spiritual ministry. She found she must just lie there and say, "Well, Lord, I will have to ask you to read my heart. . . ."

This is not to say that the Lord did not bring Mrs. Kuhn personal blessings through her times of physical weakness which proved useful in her later ministry. This area will be discussed later in this chapter.

Mental health is an important facet of our whole well-being. Chiefly it deals with our relating to reality. Can we discern and face things as they are, not as they seem to be, or how we wish them to be? Today the threats to mental health are more potent than ever before. In a civilization which keeps moving one's way of life away from the simple, down the road to the complex, confusion and disorientation result. Deep spiritual faith is a key locking in a sense of security which in turn opens up a sense of freedom. Both are necessary for mental health.

In order to preserve our mental and emotional health, we can take practical steps in handling tensions. Metropolitan Life Insurance Company, in a helpful booklet, *Stress and What It Means to You,* discusses eight ways for handling stress: (1) Balance work and play. We cannot live in a world of total work. (2) Loaf a little. The very industrious Japanese people have taught themselves to allow open spaces of time to "arrange your mind." (3) Put off until tomorrow. Perhaps we try to do too much in one day. (4) Work off tensions. Sometimes working hard keeps our minds too much occupied to worry. Doctors may be better able to judge than we, however, when this is the best therapy. (5) Talk out troubles. It is better to keep our problems out in front where we can keep a little distance from them and still face them, than to let them boil inside us. Close friends will be glad to listen. Our closest Friend is always available. ". . . by prayer and supplication with thanksgiving let your requests be made known unto God. And the peace of God, which passeth all understanding, shall keep your hearts and minds through Christ Jesus" (Philippians 4:6, 7). (6) Learn to accept what you cannot change. An attitude of submissiveness even in the face of something unchangeable is thought by some to be cowardly and weak. But it may not be the avenue of least resistance. The attitude of acceptance requires strength and will power, but it brings true peace. (7) Get away from it all. Psychiatrists sometimes recommend this solution, whether for short periods or permanently. Jesus sometimes had to leave the crowds and go away alone into the mountain. (8) Have regular checkups. While a strong religious faith does help mental health, the latter is not dependent upon the former. Factors beyond our control, including physical breakdown in the complex body machine, can cause impairment in mental health, which needs professional treatment.

Let us now focus attention on our spiritual health, which, as we have said, is closely but not completely tied up with physical-mental health. We cannot expect spiritual health without providing spiritual nourishment. The "heavenly" foods of prayer, Bible study, and witnessing to our faith are needed daily. Devotional literature should not substitute for Bible study, but can be an excellent aid.

Prayer is fundamental. Group prayer cannot substitute for personal communion with God. When life moves along quite smoothly, we are in the greatest danger of neglecting prayer. We need to form well-established habits of personal communion with God. Prayer may become routine, but when sincere, it keeps us in contact with the source of spiritual power.

Dr. Alexis Carrel, who has done 33 years of brilliant bio-

149

logical research at Rockefeller Institute, says prayer is the most powerful form of energy that can be generated. He has found that the influence of prayer on the mind and body is as demonstrable as that of secreting glands. Why are we so slow to use fully this life-giving power?

Spiritual health requires a continual dealing with sin in our lives, just as physical health must keep dealing with disease. Scientists discover cures for sick bodies and minds, but no earthly power can heal a sick soul. The Great Physician is always ready to help us conquer the disease of sin when we heed that regulator within us, our conscience, in confessing our faults and turning from them.

Our physical, mental, and emotional health is needed for the transitional experience of this life journey, which, though important, will come to an end. But our spiritual health is an eternal thing. William Law has said, "This mystery of an inward life hidden in man is his most precious treasure. . . ." Each of us is a steward of this rich fortune.

THE GIFT TO WOMEN OF AIDING THE HEALTH OF OTHERS

In a woman's journey of life come various opportunities to aid the health of others. As a mother, this privilege begins before the new life is born into the world. Women are the teachers of small children, guiding their developing minds as well as their physical growth. Chiefly to women falls the daily job of preparing food for most of the people of the world. As nurses and homemakers, they care for the sick, and fill roles of ministering to the grieving and sorrowing. Any special opportunity for helping others is truly a gift of God, a trust from above.

We plan three meals a day. Many women in other parts of the world would be grateful if they had the resources for planning one decent meal a day for their families. We choose from well-stocked supermarket shelves, deep freezers, and our garden produce. Since we are almost totally responsible for planning the meals our families will eat, and the consequences have a large effect on the family's health, cooking is really a moral as well as a routine task. Wastefulness, unconcern, laziness, or ignorance in doing this job proves our inefficiency or our poor stewardship.

Most Americans get plenty to eat, yet many are in need of proper diet. Good nutrition is necessary for physical and emotional well-being. It influences our ability to see our opportunities and enjoy our work. Good nutrition affects physical appearance, personality, disposition, emotional responses, vigor, and endurance.

Every woman who does the work of a dietitian or cook should understand the basic groups of nutrients needed daily. Nutritionists list five essential ingredients for a healthy diet:

1. The milk and cheese group. Adults need the equivalent of a pint of milk a day, children a quart.
2. Meat, fish, eggs group. Two or more servings daily.
3. Vegetable-fruit group. Four or more servings daily, including a dark green or deep yellow vegetable, and citrus fruit.
4. Bread-cereal group. Four or more servings daily.
5. Pleasant atmosphere and relationships at the table. It has been proved that without this ingredient, the four groups of foods are of little value. The housewife, after being tired from the meal preparation, may forget the importance of mealtime being a happy time, and fail to do her part in making it so.

Concerning the problem of overweight, a woman may be primarily interested in how it affects herself, and not just for health reasons! She should think also of her family. The growing children and the question of overweight may seem to have nothing in common. But they may be forming habits which will lead directly to overweight as soon as they are grown. Mothers do well not to encourage children to develop a "sweet tooth" and a thirst for soft drinks.

The main cause for overweight is simply overeating. Temperance in food is just as important as temperance in any other area. Overweight aggravates many serious diseases. The woman who helps her family develop a liking for foods low in calories does them an invaluable service. Adults need to bear in mind that caloric needs are less as we grow older.

A homemaker can help her family develop good health habits in other areas besides the choice of foods. She can encourage regular times for rest, meals, and exercise. Our bodies are made for rhythmic action. Two examples are the heart's action, and breathing. Schedules are continually interrupted, but the body can function best when there is some degree of regularity in receiving its basic needs.

Since many deaths and diseases are actually preventable, we should not neglect to take the proper precautions. Immunizations guard against many once-dreaded diseases, yet people get slack in availing themselves and their families of their protection. Many of our 37,000 auto deaths a year could have been prevented. Much lung cancer is caused by the unnecessary smoking habit. Heart disease, related to diet, can be reduced by cutting out rich foods and living more simply. New discoveries have been made of ways to prevent mental retardation. A woman's influence can reach out to help others prevent unnecessary disease and death in these areas.

Mental and spiritual health for others is also a woman's concern. She can teach her children to grow up with a proper attitude toward health as a gift of God. One of the first things a child learns is how to take care of his own body. Personal cleanliness is needed for physical health. Parents can early plant the seeds of the concept that our bodies are to be kept as God's dwelling place.

Usually the man of the house is responsible for family worship, but sometimes a woman must assume this responsibility. At any rate, her close association with her children puts her into a position of opportunity to fill their hungry hearts with bread more filling than that of our materialistic age. She is needed to help bring their souls to birth in the kingdom of God.

Next to looking after spiritual health for our children, mental health and development is primary. Argye Briggs has written, ". . . more important than good clothes and proper hygiene . . . good health care and adequate food, is the care of a child's seeking mind." Providing for a child's mental

152

development will be discussed in another chapter; so here it will only be touched upon.

Controlling emotions and providing for their needs affect mental health. In our fast pace today, the mother may deliberately slow down the family by her example of calmness. She can interrupt their live-by-the-clock lives occasionally and show them the timeless things—the world of nature, the qualities of a sensitive heart, consideration for the feelings of others. We so easily conform to the American pattern of always "doing something" and even pressure our children into constant activity, which leaves no spaces for meditation and wonder. How healthy was the experience of Louisa May Alcott, who at the age of 12 wrote in her diary one morning: "Had good dreams, and woke now and then to think, and watch the moon. I had a pleasant time with my mind, for it was happy."[3]

Women can help children to conquer fears which upset them emotionally. The fear of storms, for one child, was changed to a love for nature's beauty and power by a parent who, unafraid herself, took her child out on the porch to watch a storm. This is an example of how love casts out fear.

Through the ages women have been expected to minister to those sick in body and spirit. Nursing has been a "natural" for women. Women have shown their peculiar abilities and instincts in the role of comforting others in sickness and grief. In order to fill this role, women have had to develop their own emotions to a place of mature stability. Those who, because of Christ's spirit within, devote their own energies to helping others to be healthy and strong are multiplying their own talent of health.

Sometimes this requires the expenditure of more than physical energy. It may take some creative "scheming" to do the most for one who is ill in body and spirit. The great Christian, D. F. Andrews, once turned from illness and despair because of a flower his mother placed beside his bed. While contemplating its beauty and its Creator, he found new incentive for his own life.

We may sometimes make the mistake of thinking that we

153

can help the deeply troubled simply by turning them to religion. For those in serious mental depression, it is best to consult first with their doctor before choosing our own therapy for the patient. Some persons in the depths of depression may become more depressed by reading about spiritual things when they are already obsessed by their unworthiness. Later, when on the "upswing," the Bible will have more meaning for them. Then they may be able to see more of the deep qualities of life that were hidden before by mental and emotional blocks. The woman who shows genuine friendship and loving concern for the troubled opens the way for their return to health.

How much should a woman's responsibility for aiding the health of others extend beyond her own home? Even on a selfish basis, we must be concerned about the health of the whole world. With the fast transportation of today, disease can spread easily. A virus which was untamed in remote Afghanistan yesterday may run wild in Goshen, Indiana, today. But we need better motivation than the fear of unknown threats to our own families.

An African proverb says: "Not to help someone in distress is to kill him in your own heart." Jesus said, "Inasmuch as ye did it not to one of the least of these, ye did it not to me" (Matthew 25:45).

Biologist and Nobel Prize winner Dr. Albert Szent-Gyorgyi wrote in *Agricultural Research*, "Much of the instability of the world is due to the fact that mankind is divided into two camps. In the smaller camp, the life span of the members is cut short by overeating, while in the larger camp the life span is cut short by starvation."[4] The cattle on a thousand hills are God's. All food is God's, but we have done a poor job of dividing it equally among God's children! Does America sound like a "Christian nation" when we compare these two facts: half the world goes to bed hungry every night, ten million Americans are overweight?

Today's world suffers from more than physical hunger. The conflicting ideologies and fears encircling the earth bring great suffering of the mind. Today we are literally pulled to and

154

fro by the powers of the air, of warped thought and confusing propaganda. Women are needed to heal the wounds and scars so subtly made upon our children and to arm them with the great truths of God's working in history. A strong faith in God's goodness and a firm dedication to His service will be needed to buttress one against the crises that are sure to come. The voice and example of Christian women around the world are vital to the total witness of the Gospel to people struggling for economic, mental and spiritual security.

GIFTS OF WITHDRAWING HEALTH—THE STEWARDSHIP OF SUFFERING

How can the taking away of something good be a gift? Only when through the taking away something better is gained. It hardly seems possible that when health is the thing withdrawn, the resulting state is anything to be desired, humanly speaking. However, as Christians we do not leave God out of the picture. With God this very thing is possible.

We must again think of life as a journey, not an end in itself. It is a temporary thing, a transitional experience which we may choose to place at God's disposal, whose plans and purposes are great and good.

A tree in its prime can bear fruit, beautify the landscape, purify the air, provide shelter and shade. But a tree is not only valuable in its peak of health. In its maturity, a tree can be cut down and its wood used for building purposes or for industry or fuel. If left to nature the tree also serves good purposes. As it dies and decays, it enriches the earth for the benefit of new life which will spring from the soil.

Our physical bodies also were not meant to last forever. They serve many purposes in the plan of their Creator, and their usefulness does not end with the onset of their decline. As was mentioned earlier, the body is the womb for the soul. As our time draws nearer for our complete spiritual birth or release from the physical body, we need reminders to get prepared for this great event. In most cases our bodies do not meet death suddenly, but decline gradually. Each sickness or withdrawal of health can help us to get ready to meet God face to face.

Among Christian people are found various philosophies concerning sickness. Because the problem of sickness is a greater mystery even than death to the Christian, many explanations are attempted. While it is true that all sickness is primarily a result of sin, not every sickness is the direct outcome of sin in an individual's life. Jesus made this clear in His answer to the disciples' question, "Who did sin, this man, or his parents, that he was born blind?" Jesus answered that the man's blindness was not due to either his or his parents' sinfulness. But He did point out that the illness was to be used for God's glory.

God can cure all sickness, but it is not always God's will to heal sickness. If it were, surely He would have removed Paul's "thorn in the flesh," which we believe was a physical malady or handicap. Certainly God had the power to remove the "thorn." Even though Satan is ultimately responsible for sickness, God is greater than Satan, and can cure illness whenever He wills. But He has good reasons in not always doing so. We know, however, that in the end all accounts will be settled justly.

One's faith may need testing to see whether one really believes God can heal. This is the easier half of the test. The harder part is to see whether one is willing to accept the fact that God may not choose to heal. We must have faith to continue believing God is good and gracious in spite of the fact of this latter possibility.

While experiencing sickness, we have time to re-examine and think through our personal motives. We may see ourselves in a new perspective and need to throw out old habits of selfishness or pride. We acquire a new sense of dependence on the powers not human. We find new dedication and obedience to God. The school of suffering is not one we choose to enter, but we find its lessons priceless.

Without a doubt we all experience some kind of suffering or trouble in this life. To each of us is given a share. In a sense, suffering is one of our possessions. What are we going to do with it? Can we be good stewards of suffering?

Every Christian is a center of influence, but especially the Christian who is struggling with illness or trouble. How much better to prayerfully await God's revelation as to how one can use the trouble for His glory, than to become self-centered and think and speak only of one's suffering!

GIFTS THAT COME WITH THE CONCLUDING OF LIFE'S JOURNEY—THE STEWARDSHIP OF SPECIALIZED ABILITIES

Now we come to the circumstances which usher in the climax of life's journey. Closely related to sickness and suffering just discussed, this time of life is beyond the temporary illnesses that have come along the way and again left us to enjoy reasonably good health. Let us consider the place of the chronic illness, the permanent handicap, the irretrievably withdrawn physical strength, which will likely accompany us until this journey's end.

To some these conditions do not come until they are advanced in age. To others these trials come early in life and must be borne many years. To all, except those few who meet death accidentally and suddenly, comes some form of this period of life. We must learn how to live triumphantly with it.

The Christian woman facing loss of either strength or the use of parts of her body finds she needs to revise and sometimes to work out completely new attitudes for herself. The view ahead looks different from the point of robust physical fitness than from that of physical weakness. Time is needed in making these adjustments. When an accident or some other calamity strikes one in the bloom of health very suddenly and with finality, the adjustment may be more difficult than when conditions come on gradually.

Primarily, a change in objective may be necessary, a shift from an emphasis on what one *does*, to what one *is*. Our modern world places too much importance on doing rather than being. When we can no longer do as we did before,

157

we feel useless. Phillips Brooks said, "You ask what you can do? You can furnish one Christian life!"

Contradictory to the false values suggested by civilization, the Bible stresses the importance of being. Life is measured by our willingness to struggle, to learn, to obey, and to endure.

Helen Frazee-Bower, a full-time schoolteacher, part-time author, mother of five and grandmother of ten, was suddenly struck down by an automobile and permanently paralyzed from her shoulders down. The almost complete inactivity, after a life crammed full of action, forced her to chart a new course of life for herself.

She acquired a new regard for her being. She found, at one and the same time, that she was both a less important and a more important person than formerly. Her personal ego took a slashing when she learned that the world could get along very well without her. Yet the fact that God saved her life from near destruction told her that this was so only because He still had something for her to do. She became truly humble.

Through dependence upon others and their freely given kindnesses, she gained a greater respect for humanity. This made her a more grateful being.

In the shock and confusion of her experience, she realized with wonder that God had not abandoned His universe. He was still "King of kings and Lord of lords." Mrs. Frazee-Bower gained a deeper reverence for God than she had known before.

A temptation for the handicapped is not to do all they can do, or to not do it cheerfully. In the Biblical Parable of the Talents, the talents which were used were doubled. We may draw a parallel here to the handicapped and their specialized talents. These likewise may quite literally double with use. Frances Willard has said, "I am but one, but I am one; I can't do much, but I can do something; what I can do I ought to do; what I ought to do, by the grace of God I will do."[5]

An old, blind seamstress in France gave to missions an unbelievably large sum of money. A friend, shocked, asked how she could afford to give so much. The blind lady replied, "The women I work with spend that amount on oil for their lamps. I do not need a lamp; so I can give my francs to light other lives."

Let us consider briefly how we should face handicaps in others. Basically I believe there are two main attitudes we take. One is to see another's trouble, turn from it, and pray, "I thank . . . [God], that I am not as. . . ." In contrast to this response is the one who sees another's problems from his point of view and prays, "Lord, make me an instrument of Thy peace." The former attitude is tainted with the superior pride of the Pharisee who prayed those words. The one who has the latter attitude will ask God to show him what he can do to help the unfortunate person feel whole and useful. He will not show pity but acceptance. Mere pity is killing; true love is life-giving.

The time of growing old is experienced by a greater percentage of people nowadays than formerly. According to Dr. Darrel J. Mase, dean of the University of Florida's College of Health Related Services, by 1975 or 1980, for every able-bodied person in our society there will be one handicapped. Age brings problems as well as joys. Many people dread the coming of this period of life. The Bible speaks of old age as a "crowning blessing."

Many elderly people seem especially near to God. As companions disappear, and worldly vanities lose their pull, the advanced in years concentrate on growing in their inner lives. Paul wrote, ". . . though our outward man perish, yet the inward man is renewed day by day" (II Corinthians 4:16).

Why do we have an unconscious (if not conscious) fear of death even though we are ready to die? Perhaps simply because we cannot completely understand death. But we learn to respect God's mysteries because we trust Him.

Departure from this life is a necessity, a privilege, a good gift. As a result of man's disobedience, man lives in a disordered world. To prevent man from living forever in this chaotic environment, God allowed death, so that man may

159

live again in a restored world free from strife and suffering.

We come to the end of this transitory experience to the time of the shedding of the womb which brings to birth our spiritual splendor. Christ has abolished the death that separates us from God. In Christ we are made alive.

About the Writer

Evelyn Showalter Bauer (Mrs. Royal H.) was born near Johnstown, Pennsylvania, in 1927. She received her B.A. from Goshen College, and taught high school one year. After marriage to Royal H. Bauer, the Bauers went to India in 1949 as missionaries under the Mennonite Board of Missions and Charities. Three years later they returned after Evelyn was stricken by polio. She has written and illustrated a book of her experiences, *Through Sunlight and Shadow.* From her wheel chair she writes articles for Christian publications, reviews books, corresponds with people in many countries, and paints in oil. The Bauers have one son, and are now living in Goshen, Indiana, where Royal is teaching at Bethany Christian High School.

FOOTNOTES

1. M. Elizabeth Gehman, *Youth's Christian Companion,* April 14, 1963, front page.
2. Charles M. Crowe, *Stewardship Sermons* (Abingdon Press), p. 19.
3. Earl Schenck Miers' introduction to "Hospital Sketches," *Reader's Digest* (Hill and Wang), quoted November, 1962, p. 145.
4. Dr. Albert Szent-Gyorgyi, *Agricultural Research,* quoted in November, 1962, *Reader's Digest,* p. 258.
5. Frances Willard, quoted in "Twelve Baskets Full," by Margaret T. Applegarth (New York: Harper and Brothers), p. 177.

THROUGH *Christ, [by faith] God has brought our estrangement with Himself to an end and thereby has established the basis for relationship with ourselves and with others.*

—*William E. Hulme.*

10

STEWARDSHIP OF RELATIONSHIP

HELEN ALDERFER

THE exciting drama of life began with the creation of Eve, when God said in essence, "I now give to both of you a life-long assignment in human relationships." We also have been given this assignment. We may not always be able to choose our friends. We did not choose our families. But God holds us responsible for the quality of our relationships with those whose lives interact with ours.

After Adam and Eve sinned and hid, God searched for them, wanting to restore them to Himself. He did not abandon them to broken relationship. The whole Bible is a record of God's work to heal broken relationship.

Thompson in "The Hound of Heaven" cried:

"I fled Him, down the nights and down the days;
    I fled Him down the arches of the years;
    I fled Him down the labyrinthine ways
        Of my own mind . . ."[2]

but he could not escape.

Through God's acts, especially the life, death, resurrection, and ascension of Christ, our relationship with God becomes both possibility and by faith a reality. But as long as we are separated from God by our sins, we are prevented from becoming whole persons. And in this condition we cannot be a means by which God can call other persons out of their separateness.

Here is the basis for the stewardship of relationship; when we sense our separation from God and see the tragedy of it and by faith receive the work of God in Christ to break away the wall of separation, we become whole persons able to stand in helping relationship to husband, child, and friend.

The pattern set on day six will be repeated as long as two persons live on the earth, with as many variations as there are persons. But certain bases will never vary: Love is from God (not from within ourselves), unable to be bought or taken by violence; genuine relationship is the gift of love; to be preserved love must be shared.

Even as we rest in the wonder of the fact that genuine relationship is the gift of love, free and from God, we know that certain things are required of us.

WE NEED SOME UNDERSTANDING OF SELF

Do I know what makes me act the way I do?

Why do certain persons exasperate me? Is it because their zeal for good works pricks my lack? Maybe it is something as small as a personal mannerism that irks. Or perhaps it is a grudge for some imagined insult that stands in the way. It is easy to be irritated by another. It is harder to ask why and honestly face the answer.

Why do I react in certain situations? Is it because I am unsure of myself, not prepared for it, resentful to be in it? Perhaps being unwilling to answer this question says that I am afraid I may have to learn to accept the situation or that I am unwilling to work at changing it if that is what is required.

Sometimes we will not admit that separation from others is due to separation from God. Then the struggle to relate to others results in compulsive action.

But when we are found by God in Christ, we begin to find a sense of value in ourselves. Aware of God's love for us we become aware of our own worth as human beings.

If the Christian woman knows her worth, she is able to move toward others, accepting and loving them. This is part of the often painful process of growing up, of becoming mature Christians. For most of us the process is usually slow, but the signs of it are clear and they encourage us.

One of the qualities of maturity is to have a certain emotional elasticity that enables one to enter into relationship even with its hazards. This is the solemnity of the marriage ceremony, two persons putting their entire capacity for joy and pain at the disposal of the other. The reward, which cannot be known in advance, is finding new depths of caring and enjoying and even of suffering.

Another quality in the maturing person is that quality of being hospitable and accepting toward all people and ideas. A friend, whom I seldom think of without the adjective "warm," comes to mind. I know that each time we meet she will be receptive to me and to whatever thoughts I may have. Not that she will always agree; she has often saved me from myself. But she does not cast aside people or ideas.

Do you consider yourself a person able to trust and to be trustworthy? During World War II a national magazine carried the story of a refugee child. The child, torn from home and all material possessions, riding in a crowded boxcar to an unknown destination, was not afraid. She stood beside her mother and held a bit of her mother's skirt in her hand and was comforted through trust.

Are you able to enjoy relationships that are rightfully those of equals without trying to change them to provide some remembered childhood security? This can be seen in the marriage in which one does not try to make the other into a parent for emotional support but fulfills the requirement of mature marriage—"Two people standing up straight, looking into each other's eyes."

Sometimes we may have insisted that the difficult part of "Love thy neighbour as thyself" is to love our neighbors. But that might come much easier if we first learned what it means to love or understand ourselves.

WE NEED SOME UNDERSTANDING OF OTHERS

The acceptance of others as they are is the beginning of love's work. To be accepted and understood is life-freeing.

When we first meet, beyond the words we say to each other, we ask, "Do you recognize and accept my personality with its uniqueness?" The answer we give will have a great deal to say about the quality of relationship we will develop.

Our readiness to make room for another will help the other to be a person who does not have to be on guard, taking little shallow breaths in fear, but one who can breathe freely.

Jesus brought this gift of understanding to persons. The woman at the well wondered how it was that He saw her so clearly. Nathanael marveled at His insight into his human need. And Zacchaeus' surprise was that Jesus knew him so well.

In *My Darling from the Lions* Edita Morris said that Rolf's secret was that with complete sincerity he bowed before the inner man he saw in every person he talked to.

Martin Buber called true relationship an I-Thou relationship in which we see the divine in another. It is when we see the other person as an "it" that we lose the possibility of creative relationship with him.

When we are able to accept each other in hours of weakness as well as in hours of strength, we truly practice the command to "love one another." None of us is always in top form. We are not always the best friend in a mature friendship, or the best partner in a good marriage, or the best of parents in a warm parent-child relationship. It is good to be able to accept one another just as we are.

UNDERSTANDING OUR NEED OF EACH OTHER

God could have created only one person to fulfill the need for fellowship, but He created two, both for Himself and for each other. Then He called this act "very good."

The need to reveal oneself is deep; it is as though we have a built-in knowledge that in this way lies wholeness.

This revealing at times seems to bring only misunderstanding. Yet painful as this is, it is less painful than not to have tried to know and be known.

Only encounter with a person in particular, not persons in general, can fill this need. For instance, the invitation to attend an "open house" where there is the possibility of much talk with little meaning tempts me to remain at home. But then I recall moments of true meeting in just such gatherings and excitement kindles at the prospect.

It takes the impact of person on person for growth, too. "Love makes a man grow to his full stature." Every stage of growth requires relatedness to another. Aldous Huxley showed so well in *Brave New World* how not even modern science can be expected to furnish a workable substitute for old-fashioned relationships.

How often the hands of those we love and know best reach out to us! How often the hands of those we hardly know are stretched toward us!

Our needs, too, call out to others.

Have we begun to understand that God made us to live in redemptive relationship with each other?

HUSBAND-WIFE RELATIONSHIPS

We find life's most satisfying relationships with the persons who are most significant to us. So marriage holds within it immense possibilities. Calling one another into relationships of love and trust with God and with others becomes the highest purpose of true marriage.

The marriage relationship will have been in the making a long time, originating in part in one's feelings about one's own parents. Did we see that they had feelings of both love and anger for each other? Did we see how this could be possible and how conflict might not always be "bad"? Did we know how Mother felt about being a woman? A wife?

We will have brought to marriage some understandings of the relationship; for instance, whether it is a battle for supremacy or a partnership. In a highly competitive society we may have come to believe that it is good to win and bad to lose and so will have to learn that marriage is not a competition. A man testified in court, "Our marriage is a battle of wills," thus implicating both himself and his wife.

There is no short cut to a good marriage relationship, advertising slogans to the contrary. Nor just because much has been written about it is there a master blueprint. It is not a matter of technique, of remembering Valentine Day and birthdays, of using a certain set of social manners, of wearing the "correct" clothes.

The growth toward a feeling of what is best for the marriage as opposed to what *I* want or what *he* wants is often slow. A young married woman was heard to say, "There's him, and there's me, and there's us." (They had no children.) The arriving at the *us* feeling is a dialogue in which husband and wife reveal themselves in intimate interaction. This does not mean that one says everything that comes to mind, but that one lets no seeming come between each other. Every day there are countless chances to offer a genuine or a false part of ourselves. And what we offer will often determine what the other will offer in return.

A wife whose husband will need to be away for a week may suddenly feel the burden of family responsibility grow heavy as he prepares to leave. For his sake she is tempted to display a lightheartedness that she does not feel, so that he can carry with him the memory of her cheerfulness. For the sake of their relationship, bigger than either of them, she cannot pretend.

Nevertheless, with all good intentions to be open in relationship, there will be misunderstandings and disagreements. There may be many. And it may be quite difficult to discuss them. But to be able to resolve conflicts without either one feeling a sense of loss or humiliation, but with increased mutual respect, is the ideal. This is much easier to reach in a Christian marriage where the meaning of persons is known in the light of God's value of the individual.

When Maurice Hindus visited the Soviet Union in 1960, he observed a difference in Baptist families from most other Russian families, not only in the physical appearance of the house but in the quality of husband-wife relationships. He noticed especially the husband's relationship to the wife and saw that it made a "tranquil family atmosphere . . . that was as new as it was refreshing in Russian peasant society."[3]

In further travels in villages he always inquired whether

there was a Baptist family there. If there was, he asked if he could stay there.

Here we sense the mystery of Christian marriage and the beauty. Thielicke in a study of personality and marriage wrote, "Since the other person still stands in his own individual relationship to God, he can never be completely reduced to his relationship to me. Therefore I can never wholly 'possess' the other person. If I try to do this nevertheless and ignore his self-sovereignty, he would be destroyed at the center of his being."[4]

And so love does not grow weaker when the one loved becomes ill or old, factors that enter into the love that lasts "until death do us part." In such a marriage relationship each is able to truly become the person that waits to be loved into existence, the person that God has made him to be.

PARENT-CHILD RELATIONSHIPS

One of the major vocations of life is parenthood. Success in it is greatly dependent on the quality of the parent-child relationship. Interestingly enough, studies show that good husband-wife relationships usually result in good parent-child relationships.

Because the relationship of parent and child is often cast in the pattern of power and powerlessness, it takes sensitive parents to insure that their children are free—free to ask questions and know that they will not be punished or ridiculed. There should also be the privilege of saying nothing at all. We create this "freeing" atmosphere by what we are in our own persons and by the quality of the relationship we have as husband and wife.

A twelve-year-old boy filling out a school questionnaire put his father's name where it called for "name of parent or guardian." On the next blank that called for "relationship" he wrote "very good." The school principal commented on the unusualness of this to the boy's father. Even though the father was aware that the word "relationship" was a familiar word in their home, it was the boy's evaluation of the relationship that pleased and humbled the father.

169

Luther said that parents are "masks" of God Himself for their children. James Barrie wrote: "The God to whom a little boy says his prayers has a face strangely like his mother's."

Sometimes realizations like this frighten us. We think we must be perfect or all is lost. And we know we aren't perfect and so all must be lost.

Martin Buber has placed strong emphasis on the adult in a child's life being really there, not just being a spirit; not necessarily that the adult be perfect as the child may dream he is, but that he must have gathered the child into his life so that the presence of each to the other is established in reality. Only when this is true will "children know that they are unceasingly addressed in a dialogue which never breaks off. In face of the lonely night which threatens to invade, they lie preserved and guarded, clad in the silver mail of trust."[5]

If we are mature parents, we accept the responsibilities of our adulthood. We know that we must be supportive in the parent-child relationship. As parents we will expect the child to lean quite heavily on us. How useless to shame a crying child with, "You're a big boy. Big boys don't cry." He knows he isn't big. He knows that we know he isn't. He has a right to expect his parents to be strong, to often take the initiative.

The world is shaky for the child with a parent who cannot bear to have him contradict her for fear she will not seem all-powerful in the child's eyes.

A good relationship includes accepting our child just as he is; accepting a girl when we had hoped for a boy; accepting the almost unrecognizable muddy little boy as well as the sweetly bathed and lying-in-a-crib baby he used to be.

It includes accepting a child where he is in his growth pattern, even if he doesn't walk at 12 months, or isn't toilet-trained at two years, or is too shy to go easily to strangers at three. Do I know how to love so that I can teach my children how to love?

Louisa Mae Alcott in 1854 wrote in her journal about her father's return from a lecture tour. He had lost his only coat

170

and had made only a little money. But her mother did not blame him; she said how glad she was that he was home and that she thought he had done well. Louisa Mae wrote, "Anna and I choked down our tears, and took a little lesson in real love which we never forgot, nor the look the tired man and the tender woman gave one another."[6]

Luther divided love into rich love and poor love: poor when it expects something in return, rich when the person loves richly out of the riches of God's love to him, asking nothing in return.

Am I grown up enough to love my child freely, demanding nothing in return?

The child in a good parent-child relationship is a child who can trust his world and begin to move out from it in love. This is the stewardship of the parent-child relationship and the responsibility is the parents'.

ONE TO ONE RELATIONSHIP

So much of our time is spent in quite impersonal living. Certainly to get almost any job done with a minimum of energy takes routine which can become dulling.

Visiting a garment factory I saw the hundreds of women, each skillfully performing some specialized detail on a garment. No one seemed to be paying attention to anyone else. Was it a job that robbed them of the possibility of finding each other? Or was it possible to at any time break through the impersonal to the meaningful personal relationship?

How is it possible to move toward meaningful relationships? How can the illness of excuses—too shy, too busy, too afraid people will think one overly interested—be healed?

We will not find meaningful relationships simply by the effort of being nice to each other, neither for the pleasure or advantage they give one, nor for the good we may think they will do the other. Speaking to a fellow patient during a hospital stay I commented how kind and thoughtful I found the hospital personnel to be. She jolted me to examining my motives when she answered that she also found it to her advantage to treat them well.

171

Sometimes one is met with hostility. Then the one with courage to move toward the other takes the chance of being rejected or attacked.

There are persons who are closed to relationship, to whom it is possible to give oneself in only a very limited way. Harry and Bonaro Overstreet point out that such a person may fly off the handle at the slightest disagreement or hold a permanent grudge over the smallest slight so that one is tempted to feel he is making much over nothing. In reality he is suffering at the core of human life in being unable to establish himself in a mutually fulfilling relationship with his fellow men.[7]

Love is as "perennial as the grass." And so, deep relationships are always waiting. It is surely true that when we expect them they are more likely to happen than if we do not.

When Jesus began to teach, He ushered us all into a new place in human relations. He looked straight into the souls of persons and called them into being. His disciples have never been excused from this calling.

Beyond all impersonal encounter there awaits a relationship where the pronoun "we" is easily spoken, where the meaning of "I and Thou" becomes real. There one knows how demanding and also how rewarding is the direction toward another.

Women know how easy it is to become involved in lesser things. A house can possess. Personal interest may delude into driving too deeply into a hobby or into one's occupation, when "the main field of creativity in our day should be human relationships."[8]

CONCLUSION

A Christian woman expects to be summoned by God to responsible work. The stewardship of relationships is such a work.

About the Writer

Helen Wade Alderfer (Mrs. Edwin) spent her childhood in Sterling, Illinois, college years at Goshen College in Indiana, five years of teaching in Illinois and Indiana. For 19 years she and her husband have worked in various areas of the church's program, including a relief assignment in the Philippine Islands. This is their sixth year in Scottdale, Pennsylvania, where Edwin is pastor of two churches and Helen is Home Life Editor of *Christian Living* magazine. Their five children, ages 5-18, in kindergarten, elementary, junior high, senior high school, and college, bring them an ever-broadening scope of interests and relationships.

FOOTNOTES

1. William E. Hulme, *Living with Myself* (Prentice-Hall, Inc., 1964), p. xiii.
2. Francis Thompson, *The Hound of Heaven* (Peter Pauper Press), p. 7.
3. Maurice Hindus (Doubleday & Co., Inc., 1961), p. 125.
4. Helmut Thielicke, *The Ethics of Sex* (Harper & Row, 1964), p. 61.
5. Martin Buber, *To Hallow This Life.*
6. Christopher T. Garreott, *Making the Most of the Time* (Bethany Press, 1959), p. 86.
7. Harry and Bonaro Overstreet, *The Mind Alive* (W. V. Norton & Co., 1954), p. 90.
8. Josephine Benton, *The Pace of a Hen* (Christian Education Press, 1961), p. 65.

In him *we live, and move, and have our being.*

—*Acts* 17:28.

11

STEWARDSHIP OF ENERGY

ELEANOR BEACHY

PART I

A CHEMIST in her laboratory works to isolate a particular substance. She wants to learn everything possible about this one substance, and in order to study it, she tries to isolate it from every other element. One element may be isolated easily; another, having a strong affinity for other substances, may be difficult to isolate.

These past months I have been an "idea chemist," trying to isolate a concept of energy. What is it? What are its properties? How can it be controlled? But energy is not isolated easily, if at all. It cannot be seen as possessions can be seen. It cannot be measured as time is measured. It is not noticed as children are noticed. But it is there.

I found that it has a strong affinity to other elements discussed in this book. It has a violent affinity to time and only slightly less to possessions. Sometimes I thought I had it isolated from these two, only to find that it had united with children or relationships.

Nevertheless, this has been a valid experiment. We are likely to take our energy for granted until it is absent. We are likely to squander it until one day we realize that it is life itself. And those of us who receive life as a daily gift from God become conscious of our great responsibility.

No one can hide from this particular responsibility. I cannot hoard energy. It will be used. Unless I am conscious of my purpose in life, I am in danger of fretting away my energies, bit by bit; but if I can define my purpose in terms of my commitment to Christ, my Lord, I will have a focal point which will give direction to the way I spend my energy.

HOW MUCH ENERGY DO YOU HAVE?

Although we have no simple home method of measuring exactly the amount of energy each person possesses (it can be done technically for scientific study), we recognize that, like any other talent, some have more than others. We all know people who seem to have limitless energy. Others have only a fraction of that amount. The problem is that we often refuse to admit this fact. A person with a great deal of energy expects everyone else to keep up with her. The person with a limited amount tries to keep up and wonders what is wrong with her when she fails. Each woman should, therefore, try to determine how much energy she really has and use it as efficiently as possible.

The amount of energy a woman has is determined by her body type and her metabolism pattern. This is further complicated by the variations in the nervous systems and personality make-up of individuals.

A person who is too thin or one who is too heavy for her body structure may not have the energy she might have. For some women it isn't easy to gain weight; for others to lose weight.

A registered nurse who leads a full and active life told me her secret, which will apply especially to persons who, after thirty, find themselves slowly and steadily gaining weight. She has set the weight at which she wishes to remain. She weighs herself regularly and when she finds herself gaining a few pounds, she eats a little less for several days until she is back to her designated weight.

Those who are underweight should pay particular attention to breakfast. A good breakfast will keep your work at an efficient level without drawing on reserve energy.

You don't have to stick to eggs and cereal for breakfast.

Plan something you especially like. Foods which are high in protein will keep you going. Meat and cheese are good choices, together with fruit and some type of breadstuff.

Biologists and doctors speak of cycles or rhythms which the human body constantly undergoes. When we recognize these rhythms, we can cope with them and even make them work for us.

Research has demonstrated that people have daily cycles of energy. Some rise in the morning bursting with energy but have run down by midafternoon. Others can hardly get going in the morning but begin to pick up in the afternoon and feel like really going by evening. Then there are all sorts of variations in between.

I usually have a little difficulty getting started in the morning, but after breakfast I feel like tackling any job. I almost always do my writing, which is the most demanding work I ever do, in the morning from nine to twelve. After lunch my energy level is almost nil! About 3:00 p.m. I begin to pick up again. Sometimes I enjoy baking or doing some other housework after supper, but more likely I will do my reading then.

After you have taken a close look at your daily output, you will likely see some sort of pattern. Of course, we cannot choose exactly the hours we would like to work. However, within the framework which is set for us, we can arrange our work. This means doing difficult jobs during your peak energy level and doing routine work during your lower energy level. Fortunately the human body and personality is constructed in such a way that it can adjust to a certain extent.

A woman's life is regulated further by a monthly cycle. She may find that just before her menstruation period, she is more depressed, more tired, and more likely to succumb to illness than at other times. If she is aware of this, she can schedule fewer activities which demand physical and emotional energy for that week. If she has "the blues," she can postpone distasteful tasks and do something she enjoys.

Dr. Hilliard, a woman doctor, in her book, *Women and Fatigue,* said the question which women asked her most frequently was, "Doctor, why am I so tired?" Dr. Hilliard explains that there are several periods in a woman's life cycle when her energy level varies greatly from its normal pattern. They are during adolescence, during pregnancy, and during menopause. She examines each of these periods in detail from a doctor's point of view.[1]

During all of life a person's energy level is greatly affected by her mental attitude. This factor is hardest of all to measure. I remember how difficult it was sometimes to clean the house when I was a child. But if a card arrived in the mail, saying that my two sisters were coming home for the weekend, how easily and quickly I finished the cleaning. This is an example of what educators term "motivation."

An adult, too, needs motivation or, in a broader sense, purpose in order to find her life and work meaningful.

Emotions also play an important part in a person's total energy output. Dr. Hilliard says, "Fatigue has many faces. The frustrated, the bored, the lonely, those who suffer from inability to love or make love. The genuinely overworked. Those who try to be all things to all people. Those who live with secret fear or guilt, those who live with uncertainty."

Anger gives a person an extra shot of energy for a brief time. However, when the crisis is over, we know that it has taken its toll from our energy resources.

Sometimes we can save this energy by using it while it's there. Instead of expressing your anger by arguing with someone, use it to do some physical work. Scrub the kitchen floor, mow the lawn (if you own a push lawn mower), tackle that closet. When you are done, you may be able to reason with the other person or, at least, with yourself. However, do try to iron out your relationships. Don't let anger simmer inside; sometime it will explode.

"If you are angry, be sure that it is not out of wounded pride or bad temper. Never go to bed angry—don't give the devil that sort of foothold" (Ephesians 4:26, 27, Phillips).

Be careful that anger at some other situation or person is not taken out on a member of your family. Forestall anger, both in yourself and in your children. Don't try to go on working when you are overtired. Stop for a rest. Perhaps a glass of cold chocolate milk will give you the added push you need.

If Johnny, usually a happy child, is nagging you, look for the cause of his unhappiness. Perhaps he's tired, perhaps he's not feeling well, perhaps he feels just plain bored as you do sometimes. If you give him time and attention now, he won't keep nagging you until you lose your temper. This takes creative energy, but the end result is much more worth while than energy dissipated in anger.

Finally consider Paul's remarks to the Christians at Ephesus, "Let there be no more resentment, no more anger or temper, no more violent self-assertiveness, no more slander and no more malicious remarks. Be kind to one another; be understanding. Be as ready to forgive others as God for Christ's sake has forgiven you" (Ephesians 4:31, 32, Phillips).

Perhaps nothing can drain our emotional energies as quickly as worry. Worry about finances is common. It is very easy to acquire goods, but it is just as easy to acquire debts. It takes a stiff backbone to resist the constant bombardment of goods and services offered us. Almost anything can be bought for "little or nothing down." Then the monthly bills come pouring in—with interest.

There are, of course, many other worries. "Where will I find a job?" the young graduate asks.

"How long can I bear to work with Sally?" the clerk asks herself. "We rub each other the wrong way at every turn."

"Why don't my daughter and I understand each other better?" the mother wonders.

The first step to solving the problem is always to face it squarely. The young couple with financial difficulties will sit down with the figures for their income and outgo. They may need to limit themselves to a stringent budget until a debt is paid. The high-school graduate may need to consider the alternatives to getting a job. Perhaps she should go on to college or give a year in voluntary service. The clerk may need counseling from a qualified person. The mother may find help by reading some of the good books available which

179

discuss the problems arising between parents and their adolescent children.

Life is full of problems, perplexities, and tensions. We cannot always solve them ourselves. But the Christian has a resource always available. God cares. Throughout the Old Testament we find the writers of that time reminding the Israelites of God's care of them in the past. Remember how He led you through the great and terrible wilderness, with its fiery serpents and scorpions and thirsty ground, . . . Remember how He fed you in the wilderness with manna which your fathers did not know. . . . Remember how your clothing did not wear out. . . . Remember how your feet did not swell. It is easy to forget.

When I am tempted to worry about the future, I recall our past experiences with God. Several years ago my husband and I were planning to go to Indiana University for the summer, where he would work on his master's degree. However, our financial arrangements did not work out as we had planned. Furthermore, Perry didn't have a job for the following year, although he had applied for a teaching position. We had no prospect of income for the summer. Just a few days before we were to go to the university, we felt that perhaps the Lord was asking us to go to Red Lake, Ontario, instead and help at the Northern Light Gospel Mission. But shouldn't we stay home so that Perry could keep in touch with the schools and try to get a summer job, we wondered.

We went to Red Lake. We felt that we were going to the end of the world. Imagine our happiness when we received a letter from the assistant superintendent of the South Bend schools, offering Perry a job. He commented, further, that he had been in the Red Lake area on a fishing expedition the previous summer, and he complimented the work that the mission was accomplishing among the Indians there. Later we also received a substantial income tax refund which had been under investigation and found satisfactory.

At times individuals must bear acute or prolonged strain. There may be a sudden death in the family. There may be a prolonged illness with its attending uncertainties. There may be mental anguish caused by broken relations between a husband and wife, between parents and a child. There may be a loss of possessions. How can a person bear these sorrows?

God in His Word says: "They who wait for the Lord shall renew their strength, they shall mount up with wings like eagles, they shall run and not be weary, they shall walk and not faint. For I, the Lord your God, hold your right hand; it is I who say to you, 'Fear not, I will help you'" (Isaiah 40:31; 41:13, RSV).

WE NEED ORDER IN OUR HOMES

During my college days I took classes under J. L. Burkholder, who is now a professor at Harvard Divinity School. A number of times during the class he exclaimed, "There's *order* in the universe!" I felt he stood in awe of the God who planned the order we find existing from the minute protozoa to the great outer orbits of stars and planets.

Happy homes exhibit order, a combination of regularity and flexibility in due proportions. Behind this order there is a woman who does the planning.

I have a friend who, as the partner of her minister husband, is engaged in city mission work. She has two children. Yet I knew that she was under doctor's orders to conserve her energy. I asked her how she does it; this is what she said:

"Yes, the doctor did tell me that I must do all I can to conserve my strength. He said it was like money in the bank. As little as one has, as long as you don't take it all out, you still have some. So I am trying to bank with care.

"This is often very difficult. I sometimes become a bit frustrated because it seems I have so much I must do. And such days I work like a Trojan until my head throbs and I become cranky and hard to live with. Other days, if I can plan my strategy well (I consider a few moments lying in bed at the beginning of the day to do some planning a great labor-saver), and do those things which must be done, leaving the rest, we all are much happier."

For some people careful planning comes naturally. Others

181

have to learn to be orderly. There are a few general principles which will help those who find it difficult to keep their homes in order.

The first is routine. This means following a routine through the week. The old nursery rhyme, "They that wash on Monday have all the week to dry . . . ," made sense. Only today with our automatic washers and driers, we may choose to wash on Monday, Wednesday, and Saturday—especially if there's a baby in the house. A teacher who finds Monday her most strenuous day may wash on Tuesday. Whatever the pattern, follow it regularly.

A routine should also be established through the day. Each morning there are jobs to do in every room. Don't do a bit here and a bit there. Give one section of the house a once-over before going to the next. Perhaps you will start in the bedrooms before going downstairs. After breakfast you will clear the kitchen. Some women like to straighten up the living area in the evening just before going to bed.

Enlist the aid of your children. Teach them to put things where they belong. This is the hardest job of all, but it will make adjustment to college, to marriage, to life, much easier for them! Make learning the habit as easy as possible. If a small, energetic boy leaves the bathroom towel on the floor, it may mean he needs a lower towel bar.

Another good point to teach children is to keep clutter confined to a specified area. There should be one part of the home, preferably the living room, which can be kept relatively clear most of the time. But be sure to give them plenty of freedom somewhere else in the house. Picking up toys is always a lot more fun if Mom or Dad helps.

One mother wrote that during a school vacation each of her children spent a day "on call" for running errands. The rest of the days they were free. "That," I thought to myself, "is creative management."

Another energy-saver is a good arrangement of materials. Keep things where you use them. Review your arrangement periodically. Sometimes we overlook a very simple time- and energy-saver.

I have always kept a can of cleansing powder in the kitchen and one in the bathroom. But every time I wanted a liquid detergent in the bathroom I walked to the kitchen for the bottle. It wasn't until I received a small sample bottle of detergent that it occurred to me that I could refill it and keep it handy in the bathroom. Whenever you find yourself regularly walking from one place to another, ask yourself whether there is some way you could save those steps.

Together with regularity in God's universe there is constant change. Nothing is static. Season follows season. New growth takes the place of old.

So, too, there is constant change in the home and family. The mother with growing children will feel the need for change most keenly. Schedules must be constantly adjusted. Rooms are changed to accommodate new interests.

While children will keep Mother alert for change, the unmarried woman or the woman whose children have left home will also find it necessary to make changes. She must be aware of changes within herself and in her situation and make adjustments to them.

The temperament and home background of a person influence the way she will run her home. We cannot change ourselves completely, and I doubt if our families and friends would want us to do so. However, a true assessment of ourselves and a little modification either in the direction of more regularity or more flexibility may add to the happiness and well-being of those about us as well as our own.

Perhaps there is nothing which seems more simple and is more difficult to do than the job of the homemaker who has children.

Periodically I read of a man's applying his office management know-how to the home. I am always amused by these experiments, which run usually about two weeks. To make a true evaluation, the man should run the home at least a year or two with several children in tow. Then his efficiency will know a true test.

Carol and Dick had been married several years and had two children, Denise, 5, and Jerry, 3, when Carol got a job away from home. Carol is an easygoing type of person. She hardly notices the clutter that the children make or that she makes herself.

One day while Carol was at work, Dick decided to clean the children's room. He tackled the job with vigor, discarding broken toys, torn books, paper, and junk. The children watched wide-eyed.

When, at last, Dick had the room in apple-pie order, he gave the children a solemn lecture. "There! Your room is all clean. After this when you want to play with something, take it off the shelf but when you are through, put it back on the shelf before you take another toy. Do you understand?"

The children nodded gravely and Dick sat down in the living room for a well-deserved rest. Soon little Jerry appeared at the door, holding a truck.

"Daddy?"

"Yes?" Dick replied.

"Can I play with the truck?"

Suddenly the humor of the situation struck Dick. He swooped Jerry in his arms and held him close.

"Yes, son," he said. "You can play with the truck."

Jerry smiled. This was the daddy he knew. Soon he toddled back to his room, leaving the truck at Daddy's feet.

Not even the best homemaker has the time and energy to be an expert in every area. I like an idea which Dr. Hilliard expresses in the book that I mentioned earlier. She suggests that a woman, like a college student, have a major and a minor; in the case of housework, several minors. That is, she should have one activity in which she excels and which she enjoys. Perhaps it is cooking. She will spend more of her energy cooking and less on other household jobs. She will bake a caramel almond Vienna *torte;* and she will find the simplest and easiest way of doing her washing, ironing, and cleaning.

For the woman who doesn't like to clean, and even for those who do, there are hundreds of items on the market to save her from "household drudgery." Listening to the advertisements, the lady from Mars might believe that every box and bottle contains a genie who will spring out at her command to do her work. There are, in addition, machines which will do her bidding from scrubbing and polishing the floor in one easy operation to turning on the roast at precisely 3:15.

Advertising notwithstanding, I appreciate and use many of these products. Here, too, I must choose carefully. I must balance the saving of energy against the saving of money. I must go back to my purpose and ask, "What will I do with the energy I save if I buy this appliance?" or "What will I do with the money I save if I don't buy it?"

Any woman, whether she has a large home for a large family or a small apartment for herself, should have some knowledge of interior decorating. Simplicity is the keynote of good design. Rooms which are overcrowded and colors which fight each other for attention cause a sense of frustration and drain our emotional energies.

Rooms designed for activity can utilize bright colors (but not too many) and bold patterns (but not too much). There should also be a room for relaxation, for comfort, for peace. This can also be accomplished with color and design. Simplicity does not mean starkness. A home should have warmth as well. A home should express the personality of the family who lives there.

Materials used in the construction of homes today are designed to withstand wear and to eliminate as much upkeep as possible. Fabrics that require little or no ironing are available. In every area companies are doing research, making new discoveries which will make our work easier. Whenever you make a purchase, whether it's as small as a pair of socks or as great as the house you will live in, keep in mind the amount of energy which will be required to maintain it.

Sidonie M. Gruenberg and Hilda Krech in a penetrating analysis, *The Many Lives of Modern Women*, claim, "For many girls even the simplest housework and cooking remain difficult, tiring, and always too time-consuming, probably because they learned these skills when they were already grown up."[2]

185

In my opinion the best laboratory for the teaching of home economics is the home. I have admired the attitude of mothers who take upon themselves the task of teaching their daughters to run a home, who regard homemaking a vocation worthy of their best efforts. They transmit their own feelings of its great value to their sons and daughters.

The school can supplement this home training or, as happens in other areas, the school tries to supply the needs which the home fails to fulfill.

Homemaking courses in high school and college are helpful, but they would be of more value if they could be taken when a girl is actually running her own home. The talent and training of our home economics teachers might well be extended to the young married couples on the level of adult education courses in management, interior decorating, child care, and budgeting. Or it may be that churches could arrange a series of classes with both lectures and discussions under an able person in the congregation or community.

"TAKE TIME AND TROUBLE TO KEEP YOURSELF SPIRITUALLY FIT" (I Timothy 4:7, Phillips)

If we desire to accomplish physical work, we know we must expend energy. But how often do we desire spiritual growth without giving energy and time to it? I'm afraid we speak much of prayer but do little praying. We speak of the necessity for reading the Word but spend little energy discerning its message.

How can we find the time and energy for spiritual exercise? Here, perhaps more than anywhere, we must be stewards of our energy. We ask ourselves again, "What is most important?"

I would encourage reading various translations of the Bible. New insights can be gained by hearing familiar verses in our everyday language. J. B. Phillips, translator of the *New Testament in Modern English*, says, "As I see it, the translator's function is to understand as fully and deeply as possible what the New Testament writers had to say and then, after a process of what might be called reflective digestion, to write it down in the language of the people today."[3]

I do not confine myself to reading a chapter a day or to reading a certain number of verses. Sometimes I read a few verses over and over when they speak directly to a need in my life or when they reveal a concept, new to me. At other times I become excited about the story and move from chapter to chapter, hardly able to stop.

A practice which helps me avoid "vain repetition" in personal prayer is to periodically write down my prayer as though writing a personal letter to my heavenly Father. I learned this from reading a book of prayers written this way. Although I remember very little of that woman's prayers, I discovered a valuable technique. It is illuminating to read this "diary of prayer" later and see what has taken place.

In addition the parents of the home are responsible for providing spiritual nourishment for their children. I feel strongly that the atmosphere of the home is the strongest, single factor in the child's spiritual development. This includes the attitude of the parents toward each other, toward the child himself, toward work and play, toward the church, and toward God.

The parent will need to share the Bible with the child, sing with him, and pray with him. Here, again, we must guard against too much regularity, which leads to boredom and so much flexibility that nothing is accomplished.

"It is because we realize the paramount importance of the spiritual that we labor and struggle. We place our whole confidence in the living God, the Savior of all men, and particularly of those who believe in him. These convictions should be the basis of your instruction and teaching" (I Timothy 4:10, 11, Phillips).

PART II

THE CHRISTIAN WOMAN: DOES SHE KNOW WHERE SHE'S GOING?

It is a fact that the pattern of a woman's life in the United States right now is changing. The direction that this change takes will affect me, my husband, my children, my neighbor, my employer, my parents; in short, it will have a tremendous impact on us all. Careful attention should be given to this phenomenon.

While the church should be in the forefront, providing leadership in all areas of life, it is a sad truth that it often lags behind, literally being dragged along by society. While the number of women who are going to college and who are working outside the home is increasing steadily, the church is sounding Mother's Day praises of the "queen of the home."

A woman today has greater freedom to choose the course in which she will direct her energy than ever before. With this freedom she has additional responsibilities and additional frustrations.

The choices are often difficult to make. Before she can make a wise choice, there are a number of factors which must be recognized.

First, we should recognize that women are individuals. We cannot ignore the fact that God has given women brains and talent. With the new freedom of choice women are more responsible for the development and use of these assets than ever before.

At the same time we should recognize the fact that women are not the same as men, either physically or psychologically. While a man's life progresses fairly steadily after he reaches adulthood, a woman's life consists of stages in direct relation to her children.

After her school years, she may work. Then come the years when she marries and begins her family. Her children at this stage need constant, loving care. Shall she assume this care herself? Gradually the children grow and become increasingly independent of their parents. During the children's school years, the mother has again more time and energy for activities outside the home, but her family still demands a good share of it. How shall she divide her interests? Finally, her children are grown and she must let them go. What will she do with the years still ahead of her?

The education and employment of women have tended to ignore these stages, treating them like men and expecting

188

them to be women. There is evidence that important people in educational institutions, as well as in employment, are beginning to recognize this essential difference and are working together to find a solution. This is very encouraging.

What does this have to do with the individual woman who is faced with choosing the direction her life will take? Should a Christian girl go to college? Should she embark on a career? Does she have to choose between a career and marriage? If she gets married, will her training be wasted?

There are a few girls who go to college with the ability and determination to take on a long and difficult training period to become professionals in some field entered usually only by men. They are willing to put off marriage or perhaps not to marry at all.

Most girls, however, want to marry and raise a family. Most of them will get married, sooner or later, but some of them won't. Those who don't get married have, in most cases, the same emotional make-up as those who do. They are capable of giving love and receiving love. If this love is not concentrated on the small and intense give-and-take of the family unit, it can be channeled into service in the larger community. I am grateful that we live in an age in which this is possible. I am grateful for the love woman gives—as a missionary, as a nurse, as a teacher, taking on many responsibilities in the church and community. Her training will enable her to make a greater contribution than would otherwise be possible.

But what of the woman who does marry? Should she drop her training at this point?

If she has worked before marriage, she will probably continue to do so after marriage. Then comes the stage when she will begin her family. During this stage she will need to withdraw from the larger community to give her energy to the task at hand.

This is one of the most difficult stages. Although she loves her children, the constant emotional and physical demands nearly overwhelm her. At this time especially she needs the support of her husband and of the church members.

189

Today's young mother often does not live near her mother or other relatives on whom she can rely for help or advice. From a life in which she has been free to come and go, to be among people, to take part in church and community activities, she is suddenly confined almost to oblivion. She may have a feeling of isolation which together with the endlessness of her work can be hard to bear. Most women adjust admirably and the world around them never sees the indefinable longing they feel.

A young mother has three small children, ages 3, 2, and 3 months. She and her husband want them and love them. But he is taking on all the overtime work he can in order to make ends meet. He leaves home early and comes home late, too tired to do anything but eat and go to bed.

"How do you do it, Jean?" a friend asked the mother.

Receiving this unexpected sympathy, the mother began to cry. Quickly she wiped her eyes and nose. "I get depressed sometimes," she apologized, "taking care of the babies."

I am convinced that this mother is not an unusual case. In this day when she is no longer a part of a tightly knit community of relatives and friends, it is the church which must provide the support she needs.

If these young mothers can get away from home regularly for an afternoon or evening, they will return to their families renewed and glad to again take up the work they really love the best. Perhaps a mother with small children should take a course at a local university or join a club which has a special interest to her. Although she cannot teach a Sunday-school class every Sunday morning, there may be some church activity that she can still carry.

Many young families must economize and it seems sensible to economize by not spending money for a baby sitter or for an extra activity for Mother. I think this is a great mistake. The whole family will gain from the investment of a time out for Mother.

Church members must feel a concern for one another. It is not enough to meet on Sunday and forget about each other through the rest of the week. This is easy to do in today's bustling world, but it is time to look very carefully at how we are spending our energy. The church community is one body. Each member must take a personal interest in the welfare of the other member.

There are some women who go back to work soon after a child is born. This is a very individual matter. At the same time it is a matter which concerns all of us. We cannot say that every mother should stay home and take care of her own children without examining the problem carefully.

Why are women working away from home today? Probably the most common reason is to supplement the family income. There are several questions a husband and wife in this situation should ask themselves. Does the family actually need two incomes or is the problem that they desire more things than they really need? After deducting the expenses of a mother's working, such as clothing, transportation, lunches, increased taxes, and paying a baby sitter, will a mother's job actually "pay"? Can she find a reliable, regular mother-substitute? Will she have the energy to carry a full-time job and take care of a home?

A family's actual need is difficult to judge in a country where the standards of living are high and credit is easy to obtain. The truth of the matter is that it is difficult for a young family to get started. A home is not hard to buy. Down payments are low, but the monthly payment together with upkeep and taxes is often staggering.

If a young couple has been living on two incomes, they are often overwhelmed by the strain of living on one income when a baby is added to the family, bringing, of course, additional expense. If a newly married couple realizes this, they may be able to put away at least a part of the wife's check for the time when it will be needed.

Whether or not a mother will work should be thought through carefully by the husband and wife together and a joint decision reached. This is important, for whatever the decision, each will need the support of the other. It may help to obtain counseling from a qualified and understanding person.

It is becoming increasingly difficult for a person without advanced education to obtain a well-paying job, or, in many cases, any job at all. In the past a father planned to establish his son on the family farm or helped him buy a farm in the neighborhood. Today the farm does not offer the opportunities that it did some years ago. Farms are becoming larger and more mechanized. Some sons and daughters have interests in other types of work. In these cases the parents might look at an education for their son or daughter as an investment, just as the family farm has been in the past.

Pauline Trueblood, in the book which she and her husband wrote, *The Recovery of Family Life*, suggests that it would be wiser for a father to help his son get started in his early adult years than to lay up an inheritance which he will receive after he is established in life. If the son is interested in the ministry or missionary work, the investment would be a wise one indeed. Of course, I realize that this is not always possible.

The number of married couples on college campuses is increasing, both because the number of years spent in training for specific jobs has increased and because more men are realizing the need for higher education. Whether a wife and mother should go to work to help her husband gain this education is a decision which a husband and wife must make together after careful consideration and prayer. Many wives have earned a Ph.T. (Putting Hubby Through), but it is a long and difficult course.

Sometimes a father is offered a job which he would enjoy more than his present job but with a lower starting pay than he is receiving from his present job. In such a case perhaps his wife will work for a while. The satisfaction such a job brings to the father may outweigh the disadvantages of the mother working outside the home.

Some mothers, especially those who have professional training, go back to work because they feel a deep personal need to use their training and are not able to adjust to the isolation of the home situation. A mother with one child told me, "George wanted me to go to work. Staying at home, I

192

became so crabby that no one could live with me. I was eating all the time and getting fat."

Dr. Spock, a well-known pediatrician, writes, "The important thing for a mother to realize is that the younger the child, the more necessary it is for him to have a steady, loving person take care of him. In most cases, the mother is the best one to give him this feeling of 'belonging,' safely and surely. She doesn't quit on the job, she doesn't turn against him, she isn't indifferent to him, she takes care of him always in the same familiar house."[4] But Dr. Spock also gives leeway to the mother who is very unhappy staying at home, explaining that an unhappy mother cannot very well bring up a happy child.

If, after evaluating herself and her situation, the mother still feels she should go to work, she will need to find someone to care for her child while she is gone. The woman who can find a dependable, motherly type of person to stay with her child is very fortunate.

I have observed close at hand some of the problems of working mothers in this regard. I have seen children become attached to a baby sitter, only to have her leave after several months. I know of an aunt, taking care of two children, who favored the younger child. I talked to a grandmother who took care of two lively grandchildren. She said, "Eleanor, I just can't take it at my age."

Coming home from school and seeing the baby sitter's car parked in front of her house, a kindergarten child exclaimed, "Oh, Mrs. Drum's there. She makes me take naps. I hate naps. She pinches me and I pinch her back."

I am convinced further that a mother with small children cannot give to her profession what a man or unmarried woman can give. In addition to her work, her mind is occupied with the myriad details involved in caring for a family, her heart carries the concern of her family's well-being, and her body takes on the additional work required of her.

One year I did some substitute teaching. When I came home from work, I missed myself! There were no odors of dinner coming from the kitchen. There was no one to greet me and ask about my day as I came in the door. The beds that were left unmade in the morning were still unmade.

When a husband leaves for work, he confidently leaves the care of his home and children with his wife. I think of this when I read in the Proverbs, "The heart of her husband doth safely trust in her."

If a woman's job pays well, she may be able to hire someone to do a good deal of her housework as well as for the children. She will, however, still be responsible for the planning.

A woman who has a good supply of energy may be able to do her own work in addition to her job. She is forced to manage her time and energy better than before. A friend who works told me that now she does her housework quickly and efficiently, whereas before she worked, she kept putting off doing it. This type of person needs some stimulus to help her get it done.

She will probably need to take some short cuts in her work if she wants to give time to her children. She will have to give special attention to their needs while she is at home.

There is another area in which a woman with a home expends energy and this is the area of personal relationships. She is the one who is aware of the emotional undercurrents within the family. If she is overly tired, if she has been emotionally exhausted by a demanding job, if her mind is fully occupied with the details of living, then she will not have the resources for supplying the emotional needs of her family.

She is further expected to keep up relationships with the neighbors, to write regularly to Mom and Dad, often on both sides of the house, to remember the birthdays, to plan parties and showers, and to entertain friends.

If a woman decides not to work, she will not be able to obtain as many material advantages for her family as the one who works. It is not easy to see a neighbor have her kitchen redecorated and her basement transformed into a recreation room. It is not easy to tell your child that he cannot have a fire truck or a swing set like the one Danny

194

has. But if a mother has weighed the issues carefully and feels within her heart that she is doing the best for her family, she can accept her situation with contentment.

Similarly, if a mother feels that by working she is doing the best for her family in her situation, she must accept her decision without feelings of guilt. In either case, the working mother and the mother who stays at home will need to conquer any envy or resentment each might feel toward the other.

There is some opinion now, as the colleges are becoming more and more crowded, questioning the right of women to a college education. There is criticism of women, who, after receiving a liberal education, retreat from the world's problems into their homes.

First, I would like to quote Edith F. Hunter, who wrote in the book, *American Women: The Changing Image*: "Educated women in the home! What an odd thing to deplore! . . . What more important job is there than sharing the values we are learning to cherish with the next generation of adults? What more strategic place could there be for educated women?

"Unfortunately a widespread by-product of the higher education of women is the notion that an educated woman has fallen by the wayside if she is functioning full time as a mother, wife, and creative woman in the home. An educated woman is considered a success, on the other hand, if she is doing research for a news magazine, laying out ads for underwear, engaged in further study, or somehow employed outside the home."[5]

Second, I would say that we should recognize the various stages of a woman's life and allow her both time for her children when it is needed and an opportunity to re-enter public life gradually as her children's need for her diminishes. Professional organizations could do a great deal to keep mothers in touch through meetings, conventions, and literature and help them become a part of the working world again when they can and want to do so.

When the last child of the family enters school, the mother

again has more time to give to her interests outside the home. Asking a mother to work full time even at this point is to ask her to live under considerable strain.

A mother wrote to me, "Our oldest child is 16, but I find that living with adolescents takes a great deal of energy. In retrospect the nursing-diaper stage looks simpler, but no doubt time has clouded the picture."

If our society truly needs woman's talent and training, provisions should be made for her to give part time to her profession. Employers are beginning to realize that a mother who works part time is a good investment. She is mature and reliable. She is grateful for an opportunity to work at a job which does not take her completely away from her family; in return she gives it her best.

Her present dilemma is that often she must choose between taking a full-time job and being unable to do justice to her job or her family and not taking any job and letting her special skills drop by the way. "As Amram Scheinfeld states, 'There is a growing feeling that marriage and motherhood instead of always being obstacles to careers, may add to a woman's worth and chance of success by giving her greater stability, enriching her emotional life, broadening her interests, and increasing her understanding of people and their problems.' "[6]

In fact, I feel that at this stage it is good for children to realize that Mother has interests of her own and that she can share these interests with them. If they know that Mother cannot give them her complete attention, they are more likely to rely on themselves and also to help her.

Many men, too, are realizing that their own lives are enriched when their wives have interests outside of the home. In return the husband is taking a greater part than before in the home, especially in the care of the children. I think this new attitude is a great benefit to the children.

I do not mean to say that a mother must be working for pay. She may make a great contribution as well as find an inner satisfaction by doing volunteer work in the community or in the church or by developing a latent interest. Who knows what talent she may unearth?

196

When my son was in the hospital, I greatly appreciated the work of the "pink ladies" who played with the children each morning, making the long hours go faster. A professional woman may find a way to keep her skills from becoming rusty from disuse while she is raising her family and find the added satisfaction of serving where she is needed.

A word of caution. With the many places there are to serve and the many requests for her help, a woman can easily become involved in too many activities. Before accepting an assignment, she must weigh it in the light of her time and energy, her family situation, and her commitment to Christ and His commands.

When, finally, a woman's children are grown and on their own, she will again need to reassess her life pattern. At this stage a mother today has many active years ahead of her. If she has been preparing herself for this stage, she can move easily into giving herself more fully to the interest that she has been cultivating. A mother who has given herself completely to her children may feel useless and find life meaningless at the very time that it could be full and interesting.

She may again give full time to a profession or job where her services are badly needed. This may be the time of life when she can try something that she has "always wanted to do." This may be the time that she can give her energy more completely to the work of the church.

I am acquainted with Mrs. Mann, who gives three mornings a week doing secretarial work for the pastor of a large city church. I know Mr. and Mrs. Helmick, who have given themselves to the work of the church, serving as host and hostess at the Voluntary Service Center. Other retired couples have been able to give the benefits of their experience to the church through the voluntary service program for terms as short as six weeks or as long as two years.

There are also those women who are afraid to attempt any outside job after years of the sheltered life in the home. I was moved by the testimony of a woman who served as president of her church's Women's Missionary and Service Auxiliary one year. She told the Women's Missionary and

Service Auxiliary Council later that she had felt inadequate to do the job, but that she had also felt that she should not turn down the job because of her fears. God was her strength and she did a fine job that year.

What, then, can we conclude in respect to the use a woman makes of her life energy in today's changing world? What guidelines do we have to follow?

First, we recognize that each woman is a person with individual talents, interests, and abilities.

Second, we recognize that men and women are not the same but are created each to complement the other. This does not mean that each is relegated to the strict traditional role of the past. It does mean that each will recognize the individuality of the other. In the past the woman usually played the supporting role and will probably continue to do so to a great extent. But within this role she will find a new freedom, supported by the love and encouragement of her husband.

We also recognize the unique contribution that an unmarried woman is able to make in today's world.

Third, we recognize that a woman must make choices. We are concerned that she choose wisely, not blindly. When she chooses a pair of shoes, she may like the style of one pair but the color of another. She must choose which she wants most. This will necessarily eliminate the other pair.

So, in life, choosing one course often means eliminating another. A woman's choices in spending life, however, are modified, not only by her desires, but by her family, her circumstances, her friends. She remembers Paul's words to the members of the early churches, "Our actions should mean the good of others. . . . Even Christ did not choose his own pleasure. . . . Follow, then, the way of love, while you set your heart on the gifts of the Spirit" (Phillips).

Finally, the Christian woman will be committed to Christ. Her choices will be molded by her desire to serve and honor Him.

198

About the Writer

Eleanor Beachy (Mrs. Perry), daughter of Selma and Andrew Niemela, was born at Menahga, Minnesota. Her father immigrated to the United States from Finland in 1905. Eleanor and her sister were the first members to be baptized into the Mennonite Church at Menahga. She attended Eastern Mennonite College one year and later received a B.A. in English from Goshen College. While working at the Mennonite Board of Missions and Charities in 1955, she edited the first issues of *Agape*, a publication concerning voluntary service. In 1956 she married Perry Beachy, who now teaches in the South Bend public school system. They have a son, Jonathan, who is six. They attend Kern Road Chapel, a newly developing church in South Bend.

FOOTNOTES

1. Dr. Marion Hilliard, *Women and Fatigue* (Doubleday, 1958), p. 40.
2. Sidonie M. Gruenberg and Hilda Krech (Garden City, N.Y.: Doubleday & Co., Inc., 1952), p. 63.
3. J. B. Phillips in *The New Testament in Modern English*. Translator's Foreword, p. viii. Scripture passages in this chapter identified as "Phillips" are from *The New Testament in Modern English*, © J. B. Phillips, 1958. Used by permission of The Macmillan Company and Geoffrey Bles, Ltd.
4. Dr. Benjamin Spock, *Baby and Child Care* (Pocket Books, Inc., New York) (New York: Duell, Sloan & Pearce, Inc.), p. 570.
5. Cassara Beverly Benner (Ed)., *American Women: The Changing Image* (Beacon Press, 1962). Quote by Edith F. Hunter.
6. *Ibid.*, p. 30. Quote by Dorothy Hopper.

MONEY *is not a door to pleasurable living for ourselves, but a means of the conquest of evil and achieving the kind of life Christ would approve for us.*

—Ellis Cowling.

12

STEWARDSHIP OF MONEY

ELEANOR YODER

"IF you write a chapter about money," someone warned, "you'll offend many people because money is such a touchy subject!"

Every community has a standard of living which affects the needs and wants of its residents. Most of us feel the pressure of never having quite enough money. We are very sensitive to suggestions concerning the use of our income. It is simple to see how another might manage more effectively, but we likely have a blind spot concerning our own money management.

MEANING OF MONEY

Money is nothing more than a medium of exchange. It is an expression of the worth or value of an object or service. For instance, Margaret had been helping an elderly couple a few weeks. When it came time to settle up, the old man asked if she might not take her wages in carrots (it being easier to part with carrots than cash). "No, thank you!" the indignant Margaret assured him. "I'm no rabbit!"

A rabbit might welcome carrots; we prefer a more convenient form of exchange. Since money is a medium of exchange, it represents US. It is our time and ability expressed in negotiable form—and in this day it is not carrots!

For the Christian stewardess, money is more than a medium of exchange. It is also one of the tools she uses to share the Gospel. God intends that we use money in carrying out our basic responsibility for the Gospel. This means it is legitimate to use some of it for our own personal maintenance, but to use it all for self is missing God's purpose for giving it to us.

Ellis Cowling says, "Money is not a door to pleasurable living for ourselves, but a means of the conquest of evil and achieving the kind of life Christ would approve for us."

But this makes it so painfully personal! Yes, doesn't it? It also adds something to the daily stretching of the dollar. It lifts the humdrum to an exciting, holy responsibility.

Today's homemaker is the major spender in the home. As such we need to plan, to budget, and to spend wisely, so that there is money for the really important task—sharing the Gospel.

Consider the many ways in which we use our money. If the Gospel is our most important task, then our first responsibility is to determine the portion or percentage that we use for God or the church. The church cannot operate with the change left from the weekly shopping.

"Upon the first day of the week let every one of you lay by him in store, as God hath prospered him" (I Corinthians 16:2).

If we first reserve our contribution to God, this helps us to have the right attitude toward the income that God has entrusted to our use.

> There's a way to form a habit,
> There's a way to make it last,
> There's a million ways of starting
> And a million ways to stop:
> But the way to do your tithing
> Is to take it off the top.[2]

The amount or percentage that we give will be determined by the quality and depth of our experience with Christ. Giving is really a form of worship. We give to God as an expres-

sion of gratitude to Him for His gift to us. If we do not cultivate this response of love, our love for Christ will wither and
atrophy.

> Who gives himself with his alms feeds three,
> Himself, his hungering neighbor, and me.
>   —James Russell Lowell.

Giving our contributions is our acknowledgment that God
is owner of all our possessions and that we have a responsibility to use them for His purposes and mission. A stewardess
asks not "how little can she give, but how much can she give
and still live a respectable life in the community?"

"Every man shall give as he is able, according to the blessing of the Lord thy God which he hath given thee" (Deuteronomy 16:17).

PROBLEMS IN MONEY MANAGEMENT

Determining Places to Give

We need to remember that our dollars should go to projects
worthy of our support. A man sat on a street corner holding
a collection box. He reported that although many contributed, few bothered to read the sign, "For the Three-Headed
Orphans." Ridiculous! But there are organizations that use a
large share of contributions for administration or collection,
with a small percentage being used for the actual cause. We
may be just as unaware of this as those who donated to the
three-headed orphans. By giving through the church one has
reasonable assurance that all the causes are worthy and have
been screened for priority of need.

Money-making Projects

It is becoming more common for the homemaker to supplement the family income. If a percentage of her income is
given as a personal tithe (even though this is small), the
need to work outside the home can have an additional reward.
Someone has said, "God is interested neither in our ability
nor in our inability as much as He is in our availability." If
money represents us, then one way we express our availability
is through giving.

203

When we acknowledge the true importance of our regular and consistent contribution to God through the church, we can largely eliminate two headaches: First, we can banish the need to have repeated pleas to give to causes.

Second, we can weed out the need for fund-raising projects. Several generations ago when husbands handled all the money, woman devised other means to support the church. She raised chickens and could bake a cake and give cabbage from her garden, honestly giving of her work to the Lord.

Now the homemaker shares a joint checking account, but money-making projects are continued. Is the church supper the best use of our time today? Is it not strange that women would rather give anything—including time that belongs to the family—than to give money to the church from their own pockets?

If we really believe in the program of the church, then is it reasonable to ask the nonbeliever to attend our supper or buy sales items to support that which we ourselves are not willing to give money to?

"The business of the church is not making money but saving souls."[3]

As Christians we have more important things to do than to sell doughnuts and vanilla. Our service must be genuine, not secondhand.

Tithing and Percentage Giving

There are two opinions as to the rewards of tithing. Some tithe to prosper financially, and can give many examples to verify this conviction. John Wesley taught that religion must necessarily produce industry and frugality; these in turn will produce riches.

Others tithe to express their gratitude to God but do not necessarily expect financial returns for it. The "windows of heaven" may be blessings not expressed in terms of dollars. There are those who have always tithed and have been able to do so only by denying themselves in a financial way.

Savings

After the family has accepted the need to give a percentage

of income as a contribution or tithe, experts give us the next step in managing the family income. George M. Bowman, in "Here's How to Succeed with Your Money" (from a Christian viewpoint), advises laying aside 10 per cent of net income after taxes and tithe have been paid. This 10 per cent should be invested under professional guidance to earn interest so that it grows into a working fund. This should not be confused with money saved to buy a new car or rug. The latter is saving to spend. The working fund will be used only for the unforeseen experiences of life, or for retirement age.

Grandfather knew the wisdom of this step, but our generation considers saving only if there is something left after our needs and wants are purchased. Of course there is not extra; so savings are not usually included in a plan. There never is a convenient time to save; one must simply start. One adviser says it is incredible how unrealistic the average American can be. Few know what goals they are working toward.

Saving 10 per cent is also a good protective measure for those who would skimp and save every possible cent for the future. If one's main ambition is to have a savings account whatever it costs today, then thrift can turn to miserliness. Christian thrift includes prudent spending for the present as well as prudent saving for the future. It is always false economy to deny one's self of necessary things today in order to buy unnecessary things tomorrow.

A maiden lady skimped all her life to provide her dream home for retirement. She attained her goal, complete with carpeting and the furnishing she desired. She enjoyed her home but a few months before she died of a heart attack.

Making Decisions

Decisions on how to spend the family income and the differences of opinion between husband and wife on this matter are the chief causes for friction in many homes. It has caused many divorces, and will continue to do so. If husband and wife can agree to tithe and to save 10 per cent for investment, they are ready to resolve other differences about the balance of their income.

If Father thinks a new lamp is foolish, then buys a fishing reel, there is trouble ahead. Or if Mother buys her sixth pair of shoes when Father's only pair has a hole in the sole, an explosion may follow.

If the husband is a small businessman or farmer, the problem is more complex. Mother may want a rug, while Father chooses an adding machine or a new piece of machinery. Since Father can remember that his own mother did without, he does not understand why his wife cannot consider the business operations as always being the most important.

However, his wife has likely worked and learned to manage her own money before marriage. So she may not agree with last generation's concept that since Father earns the money, Father alone decides how it should be spent.

Today merchants discover that women do 90 per cent of the purchasing in their stores; bankers tell us that women own over 70 per cent of the wealth in this country. Mother looks at the joint checking account and wonders, "Who are the 70 per cent?" But her problem is in her own home and trying to manipulate money matters with a minimum of misunderstanding.

If husband and wife can work together as a team in deciding how the income is to be budgeted on Biblical principles of stewardship, there will be much less friction and more harmony. Budgeting need not be a tug of war but a mutual decision of what is considered the most important. There should be room for small pleasures to remind us that thrift is not a grim business, but rather a Christian responsibility. Usually one of the team is a better money manager than the other and can handle the money after a joint agreement has been made. Not everyone is blessed with the patience of small details that this requires.

Spending the Family Dollar

Leslie B. Flynn compares our spending to being on an expense account with God. He has entrusted us with money for certain necessary and legitimate expenses. We shall be accountable for any wasteful expenditures.

When we realize that we are partners with God, we have a different concept of how to manage our money. This lifts our daily spending out of the world's philosophy that we practice thrift and economy to live better. We do in a sense, but we also realize our responsibility to God and His plan for us, not just a desire to climb in community position.

We might liken our experience to that of our children. We give them an allowance and try to guide them with this thought: a portion is given to God, and a portion they learn to spend wisely—we hope. God has given us the freedom to choose how we spend our income. We learn by trial and error much as our children do. There is the painful law that money cannot be spent twice. If Junior buys a kite that breaks in the first strong wind, he cannot spend his quarter for something he later desires. But Junior could learn to make his kite; and we homemakers can learn to "make some of our kites" to stretch our income.

In this day of jiffy mixes, instant "thises" and instant "thats," we could well wish for a booklet to tell us which instant or jiffy product we can use with the happy knowledge that we are being both thrifty and saving time (that precious element that slips away so rapidly).

As examples of what the housewife can learn—frozen orange juice is more economical than buying oranges to juice at home. Instant spray starch is as convenient as frozen orange juice, but it is considered one of the most expensive ways to buy starch. However, the homemaker can use the spray product to give crispness to synthetic curtains which will not retain another starch.

Some years ago a grocery store stocked perhaps 2,000 items; now the supermarket carries as many as 9,000. Small wonder we wish for a booklet to give us information and comparisons. Often the daily newspaper does give good buys of the month or comparative values.

Ellis Cowling tells us there are two viewpoints concerning how we may spend our money. The first viewpoint considers spending for ourselves like a salesman on an expense account with his company. This attitude is that we spend when we can honestly say, "I am making this purchase because it protects my health or that of my family, because it contributes to our usefulness, or advances our development of God-given talents, or provides needed rest from the rigors of work, or increases our knowledge, or makes a substantial contribution to our spiritual growth."[4] These are all allowable expenses. The only problem is, there is no limit to expenses on self with this plan.

The second viewpoint sets a certain amount or allowance to be spent for a standard of living. It sets a dollar ceiling on each item of the expense account. This implies that within limits of our income we shall decide on a total amount which, as Christian stewards, we can legitimately spend on ourselves and our family. This requires a family budget.

We might think of a third as being a combination of these two viewpoints: budgeting the allowance but considering the questions of the first point of view.

Many do manage to live well on little by following these principles. Mrs. Brown relates that her neighbors had the same income, and the same size family as her own. Yet the neighbors had little for new furnishings and could scarcely make ends meet. The Browns managed nicely. The neighbors had an open charge account at the corner drugstore and allowed the children to indulge in whatever might tempt their appetites. It does not take a mathematician to realize the results of this free rein.

Grandfather learned to watch small expenditures. Today's family seems to say, "It's just a dime, or dollar, or ten." One family learned just how much these money leaks could snowball. They cured their lack of thrift by thinking percentage-wise. The husband bought a loaf of bread for a quarter at the corner bakery on the way home from work. The next morning the bakery sold day-old bread for 13 cents. Instead of thinking, it's just 13 cents, they began reasoning, it's 50 per cent. So Father eliminated his morning exercise and substituted a brisk walk to the corner for day-old bread. The family then began to buy foods in season, by weight, and to compare prices before buying.

There is no easy formula for spending the family dollar. It takes planning on the part of every member. The plans must be laid carefully and prayerfully. Many times the family council plan will be the best way to involve every member in the planning.

Installment Buying

At one time young couples worked and saved until they could pay cash for their wants; now the easy installment plan beckons to the homemaker to mortgage her family's future far beyond the horizon. It is very common for the family to live beyond their income, but not beyond their credit. Is this wise? One expert tells us, "Borrowing money to invest is acceptable, but borrowing to spend is idiocy." We are also advised that if our monthly payments for installments, interest, and debts do not exceed 20 per cent, we can manage to remain solvent. If we exceed this, we are in trouble.

One man commented, "Our neighbors are so enmeshed in payments and revolving charge accounts, that they can never see the end—much less have anything to give to the church."

True, interest rates in many installment plans can be 12 to 24 per cent or more. Many families may pay $100 to $125 a year just in finance charges. A wiser choice is to reserve installment plans for large purchases; borrowing what is needed from a bank where interest rates are from 6 to 8 per cent; making monthly payments as large as possible, not as small as the seller or lender will permit.

The Swindle

Not only must the homemaker face the installment buying problem, but she is also urged to buy countless items that are a bad bargain. The telephone rings and a sugary voice from a distant city asks to show us their combination storm and screen sashes.

Lucky us, we have just won a free sewing machine. All we need to buy is the cabinet.

A fish peddler sells catfish that even the cats will not eat.

The list is endless! The stewardess can ill afford to fill the pockets of these glib-tongued salesmen. Perhaps if we learn

209

how to deal with these agents, we can build an immunity to their pressures in later years. Widows are special targets for confidence men, quacks, and swindlers. There are phony health and funeral insurances, vitamin pills and diet supplements that are not needed, bottled sea water sold to prevent cancer, and land that is under water.

The smooth talker has many methods. A vacuum cleaner salesman hinted that my husband would be cruel to deprive me of his superior cleaner which could be stood in the corner like an attractive piece of furniture.

Of course the lack of money makes NO IMPRESSION! A persistent peddler continued his plea even though told we could not afford his wonderful (and expensive) product. I suspect his mother had never taught him the meaning of the word "No!"

We can turn a deaf ear to the salesman who insinuates the family will develop a multitude of ills unless we throw out all our pans and buy his wares. Superstitions die hard, but rejoice, we can now bury another. The American Medical Association, U.S. Public Health Service, American Cancer Society, the Mayo Clinic, U.S. Department of Agriculture, and the Federal Trade Commission have all agreed that aluminumware is safe for all cooking purposes.

We are further advised that no one set of cookware can best handle all our kitchen recipes and food preparation jobs. We can have an assortment. There are aluminum, cast iron, enamelware, heat resistant glass, and combinations, such as stainless steel with copper or aluminum cores to choose from. Before investing, shop around.

Patronizing a trusted local businessman is a good rule to follow. If we have a complaint to make, the local merchant will not have vanished overnight. Compare prices before buying. A local businessman's price is usually less than that of the questionable seller. If the peddler has a quality product, he will welcome comparison. But if he presses for an immediate sale, BEWARE! Time to consider and compare the real value of an item can help the stewardess avoid making a purchase that is later regretted.

The Home

The selection of a home is a big problem of money management facing the family. There is the temptation to buy or rent in a bracket above the ability to pay. One economist tells us that it is very common to live in a neighborhood whose standard of living creates a real hardship for the wage earner.

A young couple who had purchased a new home beyond their means made the wise decision to move to an older but less expensive home. They referred to this move as being from their old-new home to their new-old house.

How a woman spends or wishes she could spend money for her home is a good measure of how much Christian stewardship means to her. If we are quick to see the inconsistency of overly luxurious homes, we can also remember that there is no virtue in ugliness. "My home and its contents are my corner of the kingdom of God, in so far as material things are concerned. The home we build around us is the one work of art most of us will ever create. Few of us are spiritually so rich that we can afford a background of ugliness—if the kingdom of God is not in my home it is my fault."[5]

Possibly one of the major problems in furnishing a home is choosing furnishings in a harmony or bracket which one cannot hope to complete. Remembering that we are "pilgrims and strangers" may help us to veto the expensive choice in favor of modest good taste.

Every year brides are encouraged to choose china, silver, and crystal in a harmony which will probably not fit their future way of living. While the cheapest is not the cheapest over a period of time, neither does the stewardess need the most expensive. One husband explained it so well to his wife when she looked at expensive dining room furniture. "We want good furniture," he assured her, "but not THAT GOOD!" As a result they chose a quality hutch that fit, not upset, their budget.

"You may add pieces below your harmony, but not above," advises the decorator. The couple with the new hutch have done just that. One of the outstanding pieces of their room is an unusually large round oak table the husband found at a

211

household sale for 50 cents. It seats more than a dozen and has room for the attractive arrangement that always graces the center of the table. Few would have space for such a large piece, but it is quite at home in the couple's large room, and adds a charm not found in a matching window display.

One decorator observed that a $20,000 redecorating job is quite routine. There can be a new look without such extremes. Rearranging the furniture gives the spirits a lift. My neighbor likes to change some little thing nearly every week.

We store the rug in the attic and hang ruffled priscillas in the dining room for the summer. When frosty fall days return, so does the rug. Tiered curtains replace the summery look and our redecorating is done for the season.

The stewardess will ask herself, Do I want an automatic washer because my friend has one, or do I want it because it will release blocks of time allowing me to wash any time, even in the evening if I choose? Or—can the little girls use the electric mixer to make cakes, or will it usually stand idle in the corner while we continue to do things the hard way?

The stewardess chooses furnishings for service, not to impress the neighbors.

> The angels from their thrones on high
> Look down on us with wondering eye,
> That when we are but passing guests
> We build such strong and solid nests.
> But where we think to dwell for aye
> We scarce take heed a stone to lay.[6]

Choosing the Family Car

The family car is likely to be the third largest budget expense, outranked only by food and housing. Although the husband may choose the car, the stewardess should have an interest in this area of money management too.

Those who can afford to own and operate a new car are advised to trade every three years because there will be fairly costly repairs in the near future. But financial advisers agree that many people who buy new cars can't really afford to do so. One adviser did not himself own a car. He lived in the city where he could use bus and taxi service.

Those of us in rural areas agree that we need our own transportation. "Then not the big flashy kind," warns the adviser. "If income is small, skip the power steering, automatic transmission, power brakes, and whitewall tires." This may be an unpleasant bite to swallow if one lives in a community where a car is a status symbol. Or where two cars are common! But operation costs have risen to 11 cents a mile, while some contend that it is an even higher 14 cents.

A friend who lived at the edge of town confided: "My husband considers getting a bicycle to ride to work." Why not? We could learn much from those countries who have devised ingenious ways to carry their purchases (and children) on their bicycles. Would Mrs. America think this plebeian? I watched a ladylike young woman in white uniform pedal to work. If she could retain her poise and quiet assurance on a bicycle, so could some other brave souls.

A growing number are turning to the small compact or foreign cars as an economy measure. Since their design stays the same, they are comparable to the horse which some designer could not make obsolete long before it was paid for.

Solving the problem of choosing the family car will need to fit individual needs, but it is a challenge to find the solution that is the best stewardship for the family.

Hair and Wardrobe

The problem of personal appearance vies with the expense of maintaining a home or car. We are told that a woman goes through several phases of concern about her appearance. Before marriage, she is likely to spend a good deal of time on grooming. During the early years of marriage she can be so busy with babies, bottles, and bills that she feels fortunate to have time to wash her hair and file her nails. Then as the toddlers enter school, and some of the babyhood pressures diminish, she will again become aware of her appearance with something akin to shock. What has happened to her pre-marriage image? Mrs. Homemaker begins to spend more time and MONEY to regain what has begun to slip away.

One of her main problems or concerns is her hair. "This is a touchy subject," someone advised; "handle it in a dignified way!" Woman may feel satisfied or distressed about her hair, but seldom dignified! It is either too thick or too thin; too straight or too curly; too long or too short; too light or too dark to suit her taste.

So the hairdresser has become quite adept in designing new styles to tempt madame's purse. There have been doggy hairdos with side hanging loops and poodle cuts. Hair can tower or hang in the eyes until it is no wonder that we have lost our dignity concerning our tresses.

If the styles do not suit us, we may prefer one of the unusual hair shades to give us a lift. Eight-year-old reported this startling bit: "Mommy, teacher has green hair! She said she was tired of gray."

"Oh, John, it wasn't really green," I protested.

"Yes, it was," confirmed big sister. "I saw her at lunch time."

"Sure," added John. "She told us she has green for Christmas and she'll change to red for the fourth of July."

One who likes a change for evening or special occasions can try an expensive wig for part-time wear. This too is becoming big business. The care of our 120,000 hairs has been no small item on the budget. It is not uncommon for some women to spend $100 to $150 a year on their hair. The stewardess must carefully consider if such concentration of cash is really fitting for her crowning glory.

Fashion's bill is high; it is fortunate our Christian church does not ask as much. Consider the 30,000 Buddhist women who cut off their tresses to make a rope of superlative strength to help rebuild a Japanese temple. Today a tourist can see 221 feet of this rope, thicker than a man's wrist, and visualize those who sacrificed their personal beauty to make their religious dream come true.

Fortunately the Christian stewardess is immune to either extreme. Yes—perhaps.

Wardrobes for the family are no small item for the household either. The Browns asked an economist to check their

214

books to determine if too much had been spent for food. He found instead that too high a percentage had been spent for their teen-age daughters' clothes. Stewardship had not been the question, just plain practicability. We too can give our clothing expenditures a long hard look. Few of us would compare to the matrimony-minded mother who outfitted her daughter with 18 dresses. (The number may have grown with retelling.)

As the family grows, the homemaker is aware of the need to stretch the clothing dollar. There are several ways possible. Quality clothes are a better buy than cheap material with shoddy workmanship. It is possible to select a better quality garment if we remember that lower prices occur at the mid- or end-season sales. This is very helpful if we have specific needs, but remember—aimless bargain hunting often results in useless buys. "He who buys what he does not need steals from himself" (Swedish proverb).

A missionary friend shared her method of resisting impulse buying. She asks God to guide her in her decisions *before* she goes shopping. It's such a simple remedy, but it will help one to realize that the wine purse priced so low does not match anything in our closet (possibly that's why it's reduced so drastically).

Would it really be pleasant to be able to buy without restraint? One high society dressmaker observed that her clients outfitted themselves but twice a year, and she didn't believe they spent more than $5,000 each time. It's exhausting to contemplate such concentration on clothes. One beauty expert stated, "A woman who spends all her time, energy, and money seeking beauty will never be truly beautiful. True beauty comes from within." That's encouraging; we need not apologize for the need of thrift or economy when choosing our wardrobe.

"Economy is too late at the bottom of the purse" (Seneca).

A mother must also consider how she can best clothe her rapidly growing youngsters. One mother asks what she can do when she buys a new dress for one child and the other two demand new dresses even though they do not really need

215

them. Must they have new clothing at the same time? A friend with four girls started years ago to nip this budding rivalry. One child might get new shoes one week while another waited until the next trip to town.

"What about hand-me-downs?" wonders Mother. "These outgrown clothes would be such a help to the budget." The consultant advises, "Parents and their friends can help any child enjoy wearing a hand-me-down. Less clever parents may also stir up in him a dislike of wearing it."

Another means of saving is learning to make part of the family's clothes at home. My neighbor, who makes countless new garments, is quite skilled in cutting down outmoded clothing to be remodeled for her grandchildren, utilizing what might have been discarded. This is her area of stewardship, applying her skill and knowledge to the best advantage.

It does take time and patience to learn to sew. Plaid, stripes, and dots may not be for the beginner. A check in the mirror can show that the dots on a pleated skirt do not run true. Then follows the old rule of "We rip what we sew."

While many women discover a creative joy in sewing, another may find it a chore without pleasure. If so, she might better practice thrift elsewhere. But there is sewing in every household that needs to be done: the ever-present mending. Sally let her mother-in-law mend her husband's clothes. Clothes for the rest of the family were discarded when in need of repair. Her sister observed that something was lacking in Sally's education.

Helen enjoys darning socks, actually enjoys it. So I tried to change my attitude toward socks. A little rocker in the corner of the dining room invites me to rest a bit; but home training did not include "sitting" in the middle of the day. Undarned socks are the answer. No wonder Grandmother had a little sewing rocker; she probably never "sat" otherwise. Thus she could mix economy with rest and meditation.

Children

Perhaps we should not consider our children a problem of

216

money management, but "Children have become so expensive only those on relief can afford them," says Arnold H. Glasgow.

If we check the statistics that American children consume 190 million candy bars a week, chew 230 million sticks of chewing gum a week, drink 130 million bottles of pop a week, and eat 13 million ice-cream cones a week, we need not wonder why children are expensive.

One writer thinks that 50 per cent of the ready change in the country is cached away in the piggy banks of American children. Some youngsters feel that their weekly allowance is their just due; parents "owe" it to their offspring!

Not all parents take such a view. One mother with family finances in debt took these immediate steps. She cut the food budget to the minimum, and canceled the 50-cent allowance of her children. Howls of protest must have followed. But if children are mature enough to share the family income, they can also share the necessity of economizing when the family hits a financial snag. If a child is shielded from necessary economies, he will be ill prepared for the day when he must stretch his own earnings to fit his needs and wants. If his allowance has always been given priority, will he not feel that his wants will always be possible in spite of what his bank balance may tell him to the contrary?

However, a reasonable allowance that adjusts to the family income is very helpful in teaching the child money management. He can learn at a very tender age to use a portion for God and a portion for himself. This eliminates searching for "collection" on Sunday morning. The child gives of his own. If he chooses to give a larger portion than usual, this is his choice that can help him develop his own sense of consecrated giving.

Mother may wonder how she can treat her children just alike. "Don't try," she advised. "If you do, the children will watch each other like little hawks to be sure that one isn't favored above the other. For instance, buying gifts for all the children when one has a birthday. Let the child learn to wait for his own birthday."

This is a sensible solution when one considers that most

homes have useless toys strewn about that would have been better left in the stores, even though children do need good books and toys for creative play.

One mother thinks today's child misses half the fun of creation. She remembers the hours spent sewing tiny curtains and rugs and fashioning furniture for her dollhouse. She thinks this far more rewarding than buying all the furnishings, as is common today.

My own father showed me how to drive four small nails around the top of an empty spool. Then with a string and crochet hook, he proceeded to weave a small rope. Our eleven-year-old found the old spool and asked Grandpa to show him this forgotten art. Soon he was busy hooking a rope of his own.

Helping the child to enjoy simplicity does have value. "American parents, moving into an era of the greatest material prosperity our country has ever known, are also, whether they know it or not, facing a period of the greatest spiritual distress our country has ever known. . . . Our material glory may turn to ashes for our children unless we learn to balance it with a spiritual ideal.

"Therefore: Soft pedal the prosperity in your home. Don't go in for the biggest car, the fanciest furnishings, the most in new gadgets. And above all, don't indulge your children with them. That swank roadster you're thinking of giving your son for graduation. Don't! Children who have everything become strangely fretful and irritable. There's nothing for them to look forward to. What's life without a dream?"[7]

We may smile at the improbability of buying our child a swank roadster, but there will be many other areas of indulgence for the teen-ager. Fads can create a problem when Mother suggests that they are not essential budgetwise. In some communities one not only keeps up with the Joneses, but with the Joneses' children.

A group of mothers discussed the pros and cons of the expense of buying class rings. One mother shared the following solution she found for her nine children. As each child became a junior, he was given the choice of a class ring, or

218

watch. The youngsters chose watches, and were not ashamed to give this explanation. Even the superintendent commented on their choice. If, however, the parents have given the child a watch before he can tell time just because his peers have one, this solution would have little reward. Helping our children develop the right attitudes is dependent upon our own, as Dr. Goodman suggests.

Recreation

We are cautioned to watch our spending for recreation also. These activities can reach large proportions before we realize it. There is free and low-cost recreation in every community: picnicking, camping, libraries, art galleries, public concerts, group recreational classes, and the like.

That's a good idea, decides Mother, remembering the demands to eat every time the family passes the Dairy Queen. Or the cries to ride "that thing that costs money!" when visiting the park. Youngsters soon think of recreation and a "thing that costs money!" as being synonymous.

If the family would like to try camping, then it is well to learn to enjoy what nature has to offer in the back yard. Some youngsters have so little appreciation of nature that those in charge of public parks are appalled at the destruction these children can cause.

One winter we succeeded in attracting birds to our feeder. *Wings at My Window,* by Ada Claphan Govin, is an excellent source of help on this subject. We soon needed a bird book to identify those patronizing our outdoor café.

In the spring our interest carried over to birdhouses. J. K. Terres' *Song Birds in Your Garden* gives the dimensions for a number of houses. A vinegar barrel converted into a martin house. From scrap lumber we made a flicker house, wren and bluebird houses. It is quite as interesting to put up birdhouses and succeed in attracting tenants as is an afternoon of bridge—and of much more value to a whole family.

What canned entertainment can equal putting out string and watching the brilliant flash as a Baltimore oriole flits down to take our offering?

219

One mother tells us that this hobby opened a new field of reading for her. She adds that nothing can compare with the pleasures she has watching from her own kitchen window with the children. Every spring they learn to identify several new birds and their songs. There are several records of bird songs that are very helpful for this purpose. When the family has learned to see and hear birds at home, a camping trip will hold new pleasure and awareness.

Let the children plan their own simple picnic, which might be under a tree in the back yard. Eight-year-old wants a picnic the first warm Saturday. "Will ten or seven go?" "No, they are too busy playing house." "Will four go?" *"Yes, four will go!"* Eight packs lunch and calls, "Come, Melissa, bring the blanket; let's go to the orchard." Off they go for a leisurely hour under the trees where they spot the first indigo bunting.

Or John might call, "Girls, do you want to go fishing at the pond?" (We have a wonderful neighbor who welcomes fishermen and skaters in season.) "Yes, the girls will go!" There follows a flurry of hunting worms and the cane poles. Later they return with enough fish for their supper.

The children come in with a fat tomato worm; ugh! He is given a home in a jar with some leaves, and his history is read in the insect book.

No, recreation need not be expensive!

Wills

If the homemaker has tried to follow the principles of Christian stewardship in all the areas of money management while living, it will be consistent with these principles if she and her husband will also plan to leave a portion of their estate to God's work.

One widow divided her estate into 12 parts, with a number of twelfths being willed to church and charity.

Tillie, who lived so simply, felt truly concerned about her estate. As a young woman, she felt called to serve in foreign missions. But this had to be postponed for nine years while she cared for an aged parent. By then the board told her she was too old to serve abroad. So for years Tillie taught the youth Sunday-school class in her small rural church. Her concern prompted her to give a scholarship fund to her church seminary and to six young people attending Christian college. Three of these committed themselves to Christian service. When Tillie retired from her farm home, she gave the remainder of her estate as endowment for the church rest home.

O Tillie, the good that you have done with your income makes me ashamed! You cared not a whit for public opinion, but drove your Model T for years and years, preferring to use your money for the Christian education of youth.

We need not expect that others will always understand our need for Christian thrift. Those who are kind will label us "frugal." Others will be more uncomplimentary. But let us remember that we must give account to God and not to our neighbors.

> There are a number of us who creep
> Into the world to eat and sleep
> And know no reason why we are born
> Save only to consume the corn,
> Devour the cattle, flock, and fish,
> And leave behind an empty dish   (Anonymous).

Considering all the areas of money management that challenge us, we wonder how anyone can imagine that the task of a Christian homemaker is dull. We need not envy anyone with a "career"; we have one that requires the best that we can give in daily management. John Drescher explains it thus, "There is no more severe test than to live for God in the midst of abundance."

It would be presumptuous to suggest just how each of us should spend money in harmony with principles of Christian stewardship. Rather than criticize others, we need to examine our own expenditures, motives, and attitudes, remembering that careful spending and saving habits are marks of Christian character as surely as concern for the amount used for contributions.

Or as someone has said, "The home is the extension of the mother's values. If overspending and self-indulgence mark

221

her home, then this is an expression of what she is as a person."

When we remember that our main concern as Christians is the promotion of the Gospel, and that money is a tool for that promotion, then we can do no less than to try to make our decisions with Christ always at our elbow.

About the Writer

Eleanor Swartzendruber Yoder (Mrs. Howard) was born near Wellman, Iowa, and spent her childhood in the same big square farmhouse in which she now lives. A household of eight, with three boys and three girls, ages five through 16, fills the house with many activities that leave no room for monotony. She especially enjoys writing articles about real people and finds that writing can fit into a homemaker's schedule but not without self-discipline.

FOOTNOTES

1. Ellis Cowling, *Let's Think About Money* (Abingdon, 1957).
2. Robert J. Hastings, *My Money and God* (Broadman, 1961) (Peter E. Long—"Top Priority"), p. 75.
3. Marth Ann H. Voss, *Stewardship Facts* (1958-59), p. 14.
4. Ellis Cowling, *op. cit.*, p. 79 f.
5. John Hadham, *God and My Furniture* (Inward Light, 1958), p. 17.
6. Leslie Flynn, *Your God and Your Gold* (Zondervan, 1961), p. 35.
7. Dr. David Goodman, *The Emotional Needs of Children* (Hawthorn, 1959), p. 260 f.